TEACHER PROFESSIONALISM IN THE GLOBAL SOUTH

Bristol Studies in Comparative and International Education

Series Editors: **Michael Crossley**, **Leon Tikly** and **Angeline M. Barrett** University of Bristol, UK and **Julia Paulson**, University of Saskatchewan, Canada

---

The series critically engages with education and international development from a comparative and interdisciplinary perspective. It emphasizes work that bridges theory, policy and practice, supporting early career researchers and the publication of studies led by researchers in and from the Global South.

Scan the code below to discover new and forthcoming titles in the series, or visit:

bristoluniversitypress.co.uk/
bristol-studies-in-comparative-and-international-education

LEON TIKLY, RAFAEL MITCHELL, ANGELINE M. BARRETT, POONAM BATRA, ALEXANDRA BERNAL PARDO, LEANNE CAMERON, ALF COLES, ZAWADI RICHARD JUMA, NIDIA AVILES NUNEZ, JULIA PAULSON, NIGUSSE WELDEMARIAM REDA, JENNIFER ROWSELL, MICHAEL TUSIIME AND BEATRIZ VEJARANO VILLAVECES

TEACHER PROFESSIONALISM IN THE GLOBAL SOUTH

A Decolonial Perspective

First published in Great Britain in 2024 by

Bristol University Press
University of Bristol
1–9 Old Park Hill
Bristol
BS2 8BB
UK
t: +44 (0)117 374 6645
e: bup-info@bristol.ac.uk

Details of international sales and distribution partners are available at
bristoluniversitypress.co.uk

© Bristol University Press 2024

British Library Cataloguing in Publication Data
A catalogue record for this book is available from the British Library

ISBN 978-1-5292-4266-9 hardcover
ISBN 978-1-5292-4267-6 ePub
ISBN 978-1-5292-4268-3 ePdf

The right of Leon Tikly, Rafael Mitchell, Angeline M. Barrett, Poonam Batra,
Alexandra Bernal Pardo, Leanne Cameron, Alf Coles, Zawadi Richard Juma,
Nidia Aviles Nunez, Julia Paulson, Nigusse Weldemariam Reda, Jennifer Rowsell,
Michael Tusiime and Beatriz Vejarano Villaveces to be identified as authors of this
work has been asserted by them in accordance with the Copyright, Designs and
Patents Act 1988.

All rights reserved: no part of this publication may be reproduced, stored in
a retrieval system, or transmitted in any form or by any means, electronic,
mechanical, photocopying, recording, or otherwise without the prior permission
of Bristol University Press.

Every reasonable effort has been made to obtain permission to reproduce copyrighted
material. If, however, anyone knows of an oversight, please contact the publisher.

The statements and opinions contained within this publication are solely those
of the authors and not of the University of Bristol or Bristol University Press.
The University of Bristol and Bristol University Press disclaim responsibility
for any injury to persons or property resulting from any material published in
this publication.

Bristol University Press works to counter discrimination on
grounds of gender, race, disability, age and sexuality.

Cover design: Blu Inc
Front cover image: Unsplash / Steve Johnson
Bristol University Press use environmentally responsible print partners.
Printed and bound in Great Britain by CPI Group (UK) Ltd,
Croydon, CR0 4YY

Contents

List of Figures, Table and Boxes		vi
Series Editor's Preface		vii
one	Introduction: The Case for Decolonizing Teacher Professionalism	1
two	Study Design	9
three	Teacher Professionalism: A Global Literature Review	15
four	Teacher Professionalism and the Coloniality of Power	28
five	Teacher Professionalism and the Coloniality of Knowledge	46
six	Teacher Professionalism and the Coloniality of Being	61
seven	Towards a Practitioner-Led Understanding of Teacher Professionalism	67
eight	Conflict in Tigray: Teachers' Experiences and the Implications for Post-Conflict Reconstruction	76
Appendix		89
Notes		91
References		92
Index		107

List of Figures, Table and Boxes

Figures

7.1	Situating teacher professionalism	69
8.1	School building hit by heavy shell	80
8.2	School records destroyed during the conflict	81
8.3	A classroom used to house IDPs	82

Table

A.1	Data collection in the country contexts	89

Boxes

3.1	Domains of teacher professionalism	21
3.2	Five principles for improving teacher professionalism	24

Series Editor's Preface

This is the second book in the 'Shorts' format within the *Bristol Studies in Comparative and International Education* series. This format aims to provide clear, concise and accessible contributions to comparative and international research in education: contributions that are designed to engage with a wide range of readers, including researchers, students, policy makers and practitioners.

This book focuses upon teacher professionalism in the global South by challenging the impact of dominant global agendas in this specific arena, foregrounding the perspectives of practising teachers on professionalism in practice, documenting their 'lived realities' and exploring what can be learned from their distinctive experience.

Such work has long been a central concern within the field of Comparative and International Education (CIE), where challenges to the uncritical international transfer (or imposition) of policy and practice, especially from the North to the global South, has emerged as a core, and increasingly nuanced, analytical theme (Steiner-Khamsi and Waldow, 2012). Advances in qualitative research within CIE since the 1970s have also done much to demonstrate the significance and potential of a range of research approaches designed to document and value the lived realities of practising teachers, their professional concerns and their own priorities for educational futures.

My own research has long focused upon both of these core themes, critical interrogations of education policy transfer and advances in context-sensitive, qualitative methodologies and epistemologies, in and beyond CIE. Since I recently revisited the history and future potential of such work (Crossley, 2019), I am especially pleased to see such critical perspectives being applied to *Teacher Professionalism in the Global South* in this new volume of our *Bristol Studies* series. This book, however, takes the literature forward in new and timely directions, focusing upon teacher professionalism with a deep grounding in the multidisciplinary and contemporary decolonial literature. As the team of authors argue, the text:

> aims to provide a decolonial critique of dominant global agendas concerning teacher professionalism and to propose new understanding based on the perceptions of a sample of teachers in Colombia, Ethiopia, India, Rwanda and Tanzania ... The main arguments advanced ... are that a decolonial lens is helpful for contextualizing the perspectives of teachers in the global South; the lived experiences and material conditions of these teachers are often neglected in dominant discourses; and it is important to situate the perspectives of teachers in an understanding of local contexts and realities.

The fact that the authors are drawn from a diversity of contexts and disciplines is an added strength that underpins their collective efforts to bring Western knowledge into critical conversation with other 'ways of knowing' and understanding the world (see also Masemann, 1990). Most powerfully, the decolonial lens that is central to this analysis applies Ndlovu-Gatsheni's (2013) three dimensions of coloniality: the coloniality of power, of knowledge and of being, and as a framework for troubling colonial legacies relating to contemporary teacher professionalism in the global South. In doing so, the book challenges the dominant influence of international agencies on teachers' work as embodied in global education agendas such as Education for All (EFA), the Millennium Development Goals (MDGs) and the current Sustainable Development Goals (SDGs). As the authors point out, by the outset of the 21st century, education systems throughout the global South had in place 'a remarkably similar policy architecture', inspired by external agencies and consultants but often ill fitted to local needs, contextual realities and practitioner aspirations and priorities.

Readers will find a wealth of experience, research findings and in-depth critical analysis within this challenging and well-informed book. I hope it attracts a wide readership and that this work, so well grounded in professional realities, will help demonstrate how all involved in education can learn from contemporary decolonial perspectives and, above all, from the lived experiences of practising teachers in the global South.

Michael Crossley,
Emeritus Professor of Comparative and
International Education,
University of Bristol

References

Crossley, M. (2019) 'Policy transfer, sustainable development and the contexts of education', *Compare: A Journal of Comparative and International Education*, 49(2): 175–191.

Masemann, V. (1990) 'Ways of knowing: implications for comparative education', *Comparative Education Review*, 34(4): 465–473.

Ndlovu-Gatsheni, S. (2013) *Coloniality of Power in Postcolonial Africa*, Senegal: CODESRIA.

Steiner-Khamsi, G. and Waldow, F. (eds) (2012) *The 2012 World Yearbook of Education: Policy Borrowing and Lending in Education*, New York: Routledge.

ONE

Introduction: The Case for Decolonizing Teacher Professionalism

Global debates concerning the quality of education have increasingly identified teacher professionalism as a critical component in improving the quality of teaching and learning. The role of teachers in ensuring that learners do not miss out on schooling has been brought sharply into focus in the context of the COVID-19 pandemic. Teachers and teaching have played a prominent role in the Education for All movement (UNESCO, 2014) and are reflected in the Sustainable Development Goals (SDGs). The future of teaching as a profession is also a central theme in the United Nations Educational, Scientific and Cultural Organization (UNESCO)'s Future of the Teaching Profession and its Futures of Education: Learning to Become initiatives, which aim to reimagine how knowledge and learning can shape the future of humanity and the planet by equipping learners with diverse ways of being and knowing. Indeed, the book is based on original research funded by UNESCO through the Futures of the Teaching Profession Initiative.[1] However, much of the global literature on teacher professionalism is framed in Eurocentric terms. It is based on teachers' experiences in high-income, industrialized and predominantly Western contexts. Often missing from these accounts is an understanding of teachers' perspectives, experiences and conditions in low- and middle-income countries in the global South.[2] This means that dominant models of teacher professionalism may have only partial relevance for most of the world's teachers who work in increasingly complex, resource-poor and challenging teaching and learning contexts rooted in the colonial past.

Through the colonial experience, these Eurocentric models were often assumed to be universal. They were exported and adapted to non-Western contexts with limited engagement with local realities or indigenous conceptions of teaching as an activity. This further limits the relevance of so-called global models for teachers in the global South. Recent scholarship on decolonizing education and conceptions of education from the global South has called for a recognition of colonial and imperial legacies in education and to challenge the Eurocentric nature of knowledge through bringing dominant Western ways of understanding issues such as teacher professionalism into critical conversation with local and indigenous understandings and sociocultural, political economy contexts.

The first aim of the book is to consider the relevance of existing models of teacher professionalism for teachers in the global South. It will do this through a critical review of the dominant international literature and crucial policy texts drawn from five countries of research focus: Colombia, Ethiopia, India, Rwanda and Tanzania. The second aim is to co-create, with a sample of 50 teachers working in our countries of research focus, new understandings of teacher professionalism that are considered relevant for the 21st century. Drawing on exploratory, qualitative inquiry, the book seeks to foreground Southern and teacher-led understandings of teacher professionalism appropriate for achieving the SDGs and realizing sustainable futures for learners and their communities in these contexts. It will also seek to enhance global understanding of the issues by bringing these perspectives into conversation with dominant understandings from the literature. The book will advance the Future of the Teaching Profession debate by identifying the implications of these emerging perspectives for pedagogies and learning environments of the future, as well as the future of teacher education, continuing professional learning, and educational leadership and governance in these countries. It will develop recommendations for policy makers and teacher organizations at the national and global scales.

Our approach departs from a tradition of critique of the international transfer of theory, policy and practice within the field of comparative and international education (Crossley, 2019). Analysis within this field has long recognized the global context of unequal geopolitical power dynamics as a re-formation of imperial relations that promotes the interests and perspectives of 'international' actors and agencies in the global North (Altbach and Kelly, 1978; Tikly, 2004). Concerning teachers, this has generated critical analysis of how institutions such as the World Bank have acted to regulate teachers and limit their agency (Robertson, 2012; Pesambili et al, 2022). We are cognizant, however, that the field of comparative education has constructed its critique from within Western epistemes and has too often overlooked scholarship from the global South (Takayama et al, 2015). Conscious of this critique, the research is the work of a collective of researchers based across institutions in one UK city and five cities in the global South. It is grounded in conversations with teachers from the five countries in the global South and interpreted through a theoretical framing developed by an African scholar, Ndlovu-Gatsheni (2013). These moves are insufficient to break open the colonial matrix of power (Mignolo and Walsh, 2018) as it acts on the field of international and comparative education. The title of the series within which this book is published makes visible the privilege of team members based at the University of Bristol, a city in the United Kingdom that is still learning how to reckon with its imperialist history (see contributions to Hutchinson et al, 2023). But we aspire to take a step forward in decolonizing academic debate and research on teacher professionalism.

The material and embodied experience of global inequalities and their impacts on education systems were experienced in particular ways in 2021 when we conducted this research. We were seeking out teachers and listening to their experiences within 18 months of the outbreak of the COVID-19 pandemic. Following school closures, teachers interacted with pupils, parents, colleagues and research in new ways. Undoubtedly, this context has influenced us as authors, including through the dynamics of our collaboration. However, the disruption experienced by everyone in some shape or form due to the pandemic was dwarfed by the bloody and brutal conflict that engulfed participants and researchers in Tigray. They were living through a devastating armed conflict. It was, at the time, the most brutal and deadly conflict in the world. Necessarily, the voices of teachers in Tigray captured our attention and are afforded dedicated space within this book.

The book commences by setting out what is meant by decolonizing teacher professionalism. Chapter two provides an overview of the methodology used to co-create new understandings of teacher professionalism based on teachers' lived experiences in our five countries of research focus. Chapter three critically reviews the dominant global literature, focusing on how teacher professionalism in the global South is constructed. Two broad approaches to understanding teacher professionalism grounded in a rights-based and more economistic approach are outlined. It is argued that although the rights-based approach, in particular, offers valuable insights for a decolonized perspective, both approaches fail to adequately engage with the realities of teachers' work in the global South.

Over the following three chapters, we draw on Ndlovu-Gatsheni's (2013) decolonizing framework to consider how the colonial legacy or condition of 'coloniality' continues to shape teachers' work and professional identities. Each chapter focuses on a different dimension of coloniality: the *coloniality of power* (Chapter four), which provides a broader historical context for the political economy against which education systems in the global South have emerged; the *coloniality of knowledge*

INTRODUCTION

dimension (Chapter five), which draws attention to the broader discursive context based on Eurocentric and Western thinking and in relation to which teacher professionalism continues to be framed; and the *coloniality of being* (Chapter six), which considers how the effects of the coloniality of power and knowledge are embodied in teachers' work and sense of their professionalism. Each of the three dimensions is discussed in turn. They are used as a means of foregrounding the perspectives of teachers themselves, including their views on the learners, learning environments, curricula frameworks and pedagogical approaches, teacher education and the role of their unions and professional associations in promoting voice and policies relating to how teachers' work is governed. In Chapter seven, we reflect on the implications of this study for teacher-led understandings of teacher professionalism and the relevance of the teachers' perspectives for global agendas.

The critical arguments developed in the book are that models of teacher professionalism need to take account of the colonial legacy and condition of coloniality in education and must seek to disrupt the supposed 'universality' of dominant conceptions in the global literature through processes of co-creation with teachers in the global South. At the outset, the book does not claim to make generalizations concerning the teachers' perspectives in the global South as it is based on qualitative interviews and focus groups with a small sample of teachers in each country of research focus. Indeed, the book argues the importance of developing an understanding of professionalism sensitive to diverse and dynamic sociocultural and political contexts. By highlighting the lived experiences of these teachers, how they identify and respond to the challenges they face and how they define their professionalism, it hopes to contribute to debates about how more inclusive understandings of teacher professionalism may be developed in the future.

The research for this book and much of the writing was undertaken during a civil war in Tigray, Ethiopia, which affected the lives of all teachers who participated in the study.

Given the devastating impact of the conflict on education in the region and the rare opportunity this study provided to access teachers' experiences of the war, Chapter eight is included as a special supplementary chapter to document the testimonies of teachers caught up in the conflict and consider the implications for the profession in post-conflict reconstruction. Although several of the countries of research focus had experienced conflict in the recent past, the Tigrayan case study serves as a prescient reminder of the carnage of war and of the destruction it wreaks on the lives of teachers, their pupils and the entire education system. It also underlines the commitment of teachers to their pupils, their communities and their profession, even in the most challenging of circumstances.

What does it mean to decolonize teacher professionalism?

The term 'decolonization' has a centuries-long history in anticolonial struggles and thought. In India, for example, diverse counternarratives to the colonial view of education played a prominent role in anticolonial struggles (Batra, 2020). In Latin America, efforts to decolonize education systems and pedagogies have been led by the government, for example in Bolivia (Lopes Cardozo, 2012), and by teachers and social movements, for example in Colombia (Peñuela Contreras and Rodríguez Murcia, 2006). It has been given recent impetus, however, in the wake of student movements such as #RhodesMustFall, involving students at the University of Cape Town in South Africa, and #WhyIsMyCurriculumWhite at universities in the UK, the US and elsewhere. In Latin America, decolonial thought has been developed by scholars such as Mignolo (for example, 2011, 2018), Maldonado-Torres (2007), Escobar (2004, 2014), Quijano (2000, 2007) and Walsh (2007) and in Africa by thinkers such as Mbembe (2016; also Mbembe and Posel, 2005), Ndlovu-Gatsheni (2013, 2015) and Comoroff and

Comoroff (2011). These authors draw attention to what Mignolo and Walsh (2018) describes as the 'colonial matrix of power', that is, the extent to which dominant conceptions of the natural and social world continue to be shaped by Western, Eurocentric understandings of reality at the expense of more localized and indigenous understandings/perspectives that take account of the scale and diversity of populations within the global South and pose a challenge to universalistic conceptions (Batra, 2020). Decolonization asks us to consider the unspoken assumptions we currently practise concerning knowledge: What is admitted as 'knowledge' in the scientific sense? Who is afforded the privilege of 'expertise'? What positions and contexts are considered 'objective', 'disinterested' or 'universal'? A key concern for decolonial thinkers is to 'decentre' the taken-for-granted assumptions behind dominant Western knowledge by bringing that knowledge into critical conversation with other ways of knowing and understanding the world. This is more than simply a question of critiquing the dominance of Western knowledge systems, as expanding our conceptions of the world is also crucial for tackling issues of sustainable development through harnessing insights from indigenous and local knowledge (Cortez Ochoa et al, 2021).

Although ideas about decolonizing education are often applied to the curriculum, especially in higher education in various contexts (for example, Shahjahan et al, 2021), it is argued they have a wider resonance with how we conceive of development and policy (Tikly, 2020). In relation to an area such as teacher professionalism, the idea of decolonizing is taken to have the following implications. First, it is essential to consider the colonial legacy as having shaped ideas about teacher professionalism in our countries of research focus. That is, to acknowledge that contemporary understandings of what it means to be a teacher continue to be profoundly shaped by the development of mass education systems under colonialism and then by postcolonial administrations in the era of Western industrialization. Second, it is to acknowledge that current global and national agendas are dominated by Western thinking about what professionalism means. It will be argued that in these discourses, the term teacher professionalism is often defined with reference to teachers' experiences in the global North and that teachers in the global South are often portrayed against such understandings in terms of a deficit model.

Third, a decolonizing approach to teacher professionalism must foreground teachers' diverse contexts, perspectives and lived experiences in the global South in challenging and updating dominant conceptions of teacher professionalism. As we will suggest, this must comprise processes of knowledge co-creation in which teachers are actively involved with researchers in developing new knowledge and understanding. The first two aspects of the decolonizing approach are focused on critique and providing a broad context for considering teacher professionalism; the third is concerned with reconstructing our global understanding through foregrounding teachers' lived experiences in diverse contexts. It is a significant undertaking to decolonize an area as large as teacher professionalism, which has developed in the context of European colonialism and its postcolonial legacy over many years. It should be seen as an ongoing project rather than one that can be achieved through a single book. Nonetheless, it is hoped that the insights generated will assist this ongoing project.

TWO

Study Design

This book has resulted from collaborative research undertaken by scholars at the University of Bristol (Barrett, Cameron, Coles, Mitchell, Paulson, Rowsell, Nunez and Tikly) and in the countries of research focus, namely Batra (India), Bernal and Villaveces (Colombia), Juma (Tanzania), Tusiime (Rwanda) and Weldemariam Reda (Ethiopia). An overarching research question guided our work: How can the perspectives of Southern-based teachers concerning teacher professionalism inform policy and practice debates and decisions, specifically relating to future learning, pedagogies and environments, teacher education and professional learning, and education governance in the focal countries and beyond?

The first research phase involved reviewing the international literature on teacher professionalism. To do so, we used a methodology built upon the CoSCAR approach introduced by Robertson and colleagues (2007). CoSCAR refers to a *comprehensive*, *systematic*, *critical* and *accessible* review of existing research around how teachers and their organizations have constructed teacher professionalism, which diverges from usual academic or policy theorizing. *Comprehensive* indicates that the research is extensive in scale, focusing mainly on regional, subnational and local levels, and engaging in particular with 'grey literature' from governments and relevant teacher associations as identified by our collaborating partners, alongside refereed publications. *Systematic* encapsulates our attempts to be genuinely synthetic and bring together myriad studies carried out at different times, in diverse locations and for different purposes.

The *critical* aspect of the methodology avoids unproblematic acceptance or criticism of material reviewed, works to 'locate' the authorship, context, purpose and audience of literature, and considers diverse texts as reflecting differing political, cultural or ideological perspectives rather than functioning as simply 'academic' or 'neutral'. The *accessible* dimension of the methodology refers to our aim as authors to make the discussion and analysis of findings accessible and meaningful for a wide range of audiences, including policy makers and practitioners in the global South as well as researchers. For this work, we add the additional descriptor of *decolonial* to form CoSCADR; decolonial research emphasizes knowledge co-production and the sharing of power and decision making between researchers and communities, but it also requires that the research project itself works to subvert dominant rationalities and Eurocentric paradigms, including in the 'home' research institution (Zanotti, 2021) – in this case, the University of Bristol.

The second research phase involved collecting data from the countries of research focus. Data were collected from multiple streams. For each of the five country contexts, co-investigators provided 10–15 critical pieces of literature relating to teacher professionalism in their country's context. Some were vital policy texts that set out government policy about teachers. Understanding the policy context relating to teachers was supplemented by interviews with three key informants in each country, including policy makers responsible for teacher policy, teacher educators and representatives of teacher unions. Other literature collected at a country level sought to foreground teachers' perspectives relating to teacher professionalism. The literature provided a context to situate the data gathered from the teachers themselves in the form of interviews and focus groups.

The sources of data for each context are summarized in the Appendix. Qualitative methods were preferred over quantitative methods to develop initial understandings of teacher professionalism grounded in the contexts and lived experiences of teachers. In total, 50 teachers working in either primary or lower secondary schools took part in data collection across the five countries (approximately ten in each country). The strategic approach to sampling adopted by the research team reflected the study's small-scale and exploratory nature. Given the realities of conducting qualitative research in a relatively short time frame (one month) and the context of a global pandemic, a convenience sampling approach was adopted, drawing on the existing networks of schools and teachers. Interviews and focus groups were conducted online. In some contexts, this limited the sample to teachers who had access to mobile devices and data (although teachers were allowed to claim for the data used in the project).

The sampling approach was also purposive. The general criteria for selecting teachers was that they should be classroom teachers working in the basic education cycle (either at primary or secondary level) and working in challenging teaching and learning contexts. However, how 'challenging teaching and learning contexts' were defined differed between country contexts. Across all countries, the teachers were located in resource-poor rural or urban environments, often with large classes representing diverse learning needs. In all cases, they had experienced significant periods of school closures and the challenge of teaching remotely in contexts with varying but generally limited access to appropriate technology and data. Country teams were asked to identify one or two particularly salient contextual factors that helped to define the nature of the challenges faced by teachers in each country and to select teachers who were known to face these challenges.

- In the case of Rwanda, a particular challenge identified was teaching through the medium of English in settings where the vast majority of learners and many teachers had very low levels of English proficiency.
- In India's case, the challenge identified was the use of online learning in the context of the COVID-19 pandemic.

- In Tanzania, the main contextual issue addressed was the curriculum's relevance to the learners' backgrounds.
- In Colombia, teachers were chosen from a broad spectrum of regions. Two particular challenges identified were the presence of various illegal armed actors in rural school environments and regions with significant numbers of refugees from Venezuela.
- In Ethiopia, the challenge was the ongoing armed conflict in the Tigray region, where all teachers who participated in the study were located.

The sampling approach allowed the team to develop a more nuanced and contextualized understanding of the impact of these specific challenges on teachers' professional activities and identities. As is evident from the discussion of the data, these challenges often impacted on the teachers' perspectives on teacher professionalism not only in the specific country but across several countries of research focus. This emerging understanding of teacher professionalism, although not generalizable, can provide rich insights into teachers' lived experiences and can act as one basis for further research.

A thematic and iterative approach to data analysis was adopted in which country teams first coded and organized the data according to the research questions. Adopting an iterative approach allowed the research questions to be adapted as necessary. One example of this included a question focusing on the impact of the COVID pandemic on teachers' understanding of their work and their role. The country data were then synthesized through an iterative process involving country teams reporting and discussing their findings among the entire team. This allowed for the initial identification of emerging themes. Following this initial data collection period and analysis, 40 teachers from four countries participated in two online discussion events, with one event pairing Tanzanian and Indian participant teachers and the other pairing Rwandan and Colombian participant teachers, with translation into Spanish. Participant teachers from Ethiopia could not participate in the discussions due to a communications blackout in Tigray imposed by the Ethiopian government in June 2021 (UNOCHA, 2021).

COVID-19: the environment for writing

This book was conceptualized, researched and written in 2021, more than a year into the global COVID-19 pandemic, when earlier hopes that a 'return to normal' would be possible were subsiding, and new waves and variants of the virus continued to challenge the global North and South alike. COVID-related school closures throughout 2020 and 2021 have seriously impacted education: UNESCO/UIS (2021) estimated that in 2020 alone, children worldwide lost between 41 and 68 per cent of their usual teacher contact hours – a concerning development, especially for countries previously on a trajectory to meet SDG4 targets. Without interventions, dropouts are expected to skyrocket as families cope with the economic shocks brought on by the pandemic, and international organizations are projecting drastic increases in hunger and malnutrition (FAO, 2020), worsened mental health, child labour (UNICEF, 2020), child, early and forced marriage (World Vision, 2020), and other forms of abuse, neglect and exploitation (Cameron, 2021). During the initial lockdowns of 2020, teachers experienced a rapid and largely unsupported revision of their professional roles. Where internet connectivity and devices were widely available, many teachers shifted to online teaching. But an estimated 463 million children, or one-third of children impacted by school closures, could not access online learning. Of that group, three-quarters come from rural and/or impoverished households (UNICEF, 2020). Teachers in those communities, often lacking devices and connectivity, supported their learners in additional ways, distributing materials via report packets, WhatsApp chats or socially distant in-person meetings, often supporting government-sponsored radio and television lesson broadcasts.

For the research team and participant teachers, policy makers and education stakeholders, it is impossible to envision a future untouched by the pandemic. By mid-2021, schoolchildren across global contexts remained in flux, with various combinations of in-person and distance learning present even within single country contexts.

It is essential to recognize the dire humanitarian crisis facing many of the teachers who gave up their time to participate in the construction of this document, demonstrating the many and often extreme environmental challenges that teachers in the global South face in addition to the pressures exacerbated by the COVID-19 pandemic. The research was guided by clear ethical guidelines agreed by the research team. These include the informed consent of teachers taking part; the right to withdraw from the research at any time, the right to anonymity; the right to participate using a language that they feel able to communicate in freely; the right to verify the emerging data as being an accurate reflection of their views; the right to have their participation remunerated as recognition of their expertise and opportunity costs forgone; and that no harm should come to teachers participating in the research.

THREE

Teacher Professionalism: A Global Literature Review

This chapter outlines how teacher professionalism is understood in the global literature, focusing on how teacher professionalism in the global South is constructed. Two broad approaches can be identified. One is a rights-based approach in which UNESCO, the International Labour Organization (ILO) and global teachers' organizations such as Education International and many other international non-governmental organizations (INGOs) are aligned. Within this tradition, the idea of teacher professionalism as a means to advance the right to education for all has been developed, most recently in the context of the adoption of the SDGs, and SDG4 (the education SDG) in particular. The World Bank advances the second and arguably more dominant discourse that is more economistic in orientation. As we will see, it features heavily in national discourses about teacher professionalism as well as literature on teacher motivation and accountability and the role of para-teachers. Here, teacher professionalism, where it is acknowledged as a legitimate concern, is equated primarily with teacher effectiveness. Within both discourses, teacher professionalism is seen as a critical component in improving the quality of education, albeit in relation to contrasting views of what a good-quality education might entail. As will be discussed, while the rights-based approach, in particular, offers valuable insights into teacher professionalism in the global South, both approaches can be critiqued from a decolonizing

15

perspective. We then turn to a third perspective on teacher professionalism that is oriented by a social justice rationale, showing how this is aligned with a decolonizing agenda.

Defining teacher professionalism

Professionalism is a fluid, malleable term highly contested in the literature. Generally, teacher professionalism is most commonly associated with autonomy and control over work, ethical conduct, subject/specialized knowledge and certification, and standards for controlling entrance into a profession (Govender et al, 2016). In the words of Furlong and colleagues (2000, cited in Sachs, 2001, p 150):

> The three concepts of knowledge, autonomy and responsibility central to a traditional notion of professionalism, are often seen as interrelated. It is because professionals face complex and unpredictable situations that they need a specialised body of knowledge; if they are to apply that knowledge, it is argued that they need the autonomy to make their own judgements. Given that they have autonomy, it is essential that they act with responsibility – collectively they need to develop appropriate professional values.

Comparisons of teaching with other professions, such as medicine and law, according to these essential markers of professionalism, have led some commentators to describe teaching as a 'semi-profession' (Etzoini, 1969). As Goodwin (2020, p 6) has recently argued, 'these perceptions have their roots in long-held perceptions of teaching as a low status ... technically simple work that attracts the least capable candidates ... most of whom are women'. She notes that, 'moreover, teachers are typically paid less than in professions requiring similar levels of education ... plus they work with young people who are politically powerless and therefore discountable'.

Findings from this research suggest that many teachers work in material classroom environments that are not conducive to student learning or teacher professional practice. Johnson and colleagues (2000) commented that teachers conforming with dominant Western conceptualizations of professionalism are generally found within professional education systems of high-income countries. Evans (2008, p 26) defines teacher professionalism, recognizing the subjective and situated nature of professionalism, describing it as 'an ideologically-, attitudinally-, intellectually- and epistemologically-based stance on the part of an individual, in relation to the practice of the profession to which s/he belongs, and which influences her/his professional practice'. When a group of individual teachers shares an understanding of the ideologies, attitudes, knowledge and approaches to practices that are valued, they reflect a collective professionalism. But even within this definition, there are questions of power: who decides what is valued, and whose approach is supported by the weight of policy? Do teachers' understandings of professionalism align with those evident in government policy, and do they have a voice, via unions or other representatives, in the construction of the policy? Or, perhaps more commonly, are the contours of their work lives – their pay, workloads, responsibilities, pedagogies and practices – decided by stakeholders outside the profession? As we will see, these questions are handled quite differently depending on the overall approach to professionalism adopted.

A rights-based approach to teacher professionalism

An early and significant construction of teacher professionalism for the global South appears in the 1966 ILO/UNESCO *Recommendation Concerning the Status of Teachers*, which provided international standards meant to guide 'the most important professional, social, ethical, and material concerns of teachers' (ILO/UNESCO, 1966, p 8). This Recommendation, later updated in 1997 to consider personnel in higher education settings, provided a comprehensive stance on teacher professionalism. As can be seen, the definition draws on the three interrelated characteristics most commonly associated with professionalism (Furlong et al, 2000, p 9), namely knowledge, autonomy and responsibility:

> Teaching should be regarded as a profession: it is a form of public service which 'requires teachers' expert knowledge' and specialised skills, acquired and maintained through rigorous and continuing study; it also calls for a sense of personal and corporate responsibility for the education and welfare of the pupils in their charge.

As a profession, then, it is also expected that teacher organizations, such as unions, 'should be associated with the determination of educational policy' (Furlong et al, 2000, p 22), indicating that teachers have an explicit role in deciding the conditions of their work. As such, it reflects the era during which it was written, when global North teachers enjoyed a substantial measure of professional autonomy. Grace (1987, p 209) indicated that in the two decades following World War II, organized teachers 'had a strong sense that they were partners in the great educational enterprise' and were vital in restructuring education during that period. For Hargreaves (2000), this period was one of 'autonomous' or 'collegial' professionalism; for Dale (1989), it was one of 'licensed autonomy' in which teachers enjoyed pedagogic freedom and held considerable influence in curriculum development and implementation, granting them increased social recognition and expertise-driven status. Teachers' expertise was described as pedagogic content knowledge, bringing together subject and knowledge on how to teach that subject (Bullough, 2001; Shulman, 2011). Classroom researchers called attention to the reflexive nature of teachers' professional expertise, as teachers continuously reflect on and adjust their practice according to learners' responses (Connelly and Clandinin, 1990; Schon, 1991). Other researchers stressed the personal nature of teachers' work, as they drew on their physical, emotional and creative resources in their interpersonal relations with children and young people (Nias, 1989; Woods and Jeffrey, 2002).

During this same era, many formerly colonized nations were becoming independent, and education was seen as a vehicle towards national development. Many countries in the global South, including the countries of research focus, sought to expand their education systems. In many instances, teachers were accorded professional status, including being employed as civil servants, subject to professional standards and entry requirements (for example, Welmond, 2002). At the same time, they were called upon to make sacrifices in the service of nation building by accepting postings in underserved areas where working conditions, living conditions and opportunities for continuing development diverged sharply from those assumed by Western models of professionalism (Barrett, 2008).

If the Recommendation was based more on aspiration than on reality when it was adopted, in the decades since, its power and promise have become ever more diminished. During the era of structural adjustment programmes in the global South, teachers' remuneration and pensions were significant targets for cuts and reforms (ILO, 1996), degrading the social capital of the profession and relegating it as an unattractive career. Today, the Recommendation reflects a drastically different international context, and even as countries remain signatories, a host of modern economic, social and environmental factors have dramatically changed the context in which education systems operate, placing new demands on the work of schools and teachers.

The 2015 Sustainable Development Goals agenda also has profound implications for understanding teacher professionalism. Whereas priority was afforded under the MDGs to increase access to basic education, SDG4 builds on the Education for All goals to aim for inclusive and good-quality education within a lifelong learning framework. Goal 4.7 signals a repurposing of education to support sustainable development and global citizenship. The centrality of teachers is emphasized in the text to target 4C, which calls for expanding the teaching workforce in the South and acknowledges that 'teachers are a fundamental condition for guaranteeing quality education … [and] should be empowered, adequately recruited and remunerated, motivated, professionally qualified, and supported within well-resourced, efficient and effectively governed systems'. The view of a good-quality education implicit in the SDG discourse can be seen to build on earlier UNESCO discourses relating to the quality of education (UNESCO, 2004). It encompasses a range of cognitive and affective outcomes from basic literacy and numeracy to more advanced technical/vocational skills. It also encompasses citizenship and environmental education required for achieving sustainable livelihoods.

More recently, UNESCO has renewed its interest in teacher professionalism. This is exemplified by the development of the global teachers' union, Education International, and of a Global Framework of Professional Teaching Standards (UNESCO/EI, 2019). The standards are intended to be adopted by teachers' organizations and governments in different country contexts. They are organized according to three key domains, which are included in Box 3.1. It will be argued in later sections that the domains provide a helpful way of framing teachers' perspectives on key aspects of teacher professionalism. It will also be suggested, however, that teachers' perspectives add nuance and contextualized understanding to the standards as they are currently set out under each domain.

The definitions of each of these domains represent the understanding of teachers' professional expertise, including knowledge of learners, subject content and pedagogy. However, it falls short of recognizing the dynamic, reflexive, constantly evolving nature of teachers' expertise and knowledge that has characterized the rights-based approach and the importance of context, to which we will return in the conclusion of the book (Chapter seven).

Box 3.1: Domains of teacher professionalism

1. Teaching knowledge and understanding

It can be taken as given that effective teaching relies on teachers being expert enough at the knowledge, skills and understandings of particular subjects or learning areas to be able to teach them. Good teachers know and understand their subjects, teaching methodologies and students. Teachers also understand the social, cultural and developmental issues that might relate to their students and their learning processes. Specific learning content will vary substantially across countries, but teaching will always require enough depth of knowledge, skills and understanding of content, the students in the class and contextual issues to be able to bring the students to their own appropriate levels of understanding.

This should not imply that teaching is a simple process of transmitting knowledge from a teacher to a student. Meaning and understanding is developed in processes and relationships shaped by the complex and varied contexts within which students learn. There is therefore a substantial overlap in real terms with the other essential domains of this framework.

2. Teaching practice

The standards in this domain describe the key dimensions of the direct engagement of teachers with their students. Effective teaching is crucially determined in this domain, where the practices that most distinctly constitute teaching can be elaborated. Teaching activities manifest in innumerable ways and always reflect a teacher's ambition for, and understanding of, student learning, welfare and development. Effective teaching methodologies and practices within this domain rely on knowledge and understanding as well as on various teaching relations.

3. Teaching relations

Teaching is inherently constituted in relationships. As well as engaging with students, professional relationships with colleagues, parents, caregivers and education authorities are crucial to effective teaching. Relations with the general community are also crucial to a teacher's work and to the profession as a whole.

Source: UNESCO/EI (2019)

The World Bank and management-driven professionalism

Since the 1980s, there has been a significant change in the discourse around teacher professionalism in the global North. In contrast with the member–driven professionalism advocated by the 1966 Recommendation, Robertson (2012, p 586) notes how policy makers' neoliberal, managerial ideology worked to 'colonise the field of symbolic control' over the teaching profession, redefining the work of teachers. A professional teacher, rather than displaying the responsibility, autonomy and knowledge called for in earlier professional constructions, is instead a worker who responds to the dictates of policy and management. Increasing rigidity and top-down directives for the curriculum, pedagogy and medium of instruction means that teachers have less freedom to operate within their classrooms as their performance is judged according to externally constructed and imposed standards, rather than emerging from the teachers' professional collective. Accountability is framed not as professional accountability to the larger professional service body, perhaps evident in medical or legal fields, but to 'market-based competition and increased surveillance' (Whitty, 2008, p 34).

Professional teachers, then, are reframed in these discourses as corporate employees, functioning according to a service agreement and producing desired outcomes (Evans, 2008), with school leaders like principals or head teachers acting more as managers than senior academic colleagues. This form of professionalism has been labelled as managerial, measured, performative or prescriptive professionalism discourses (Sachs, 2001; Robertson et al, 2007; Ball, 2008, 2015), with Dale's (1989) 'licensed autonomy' becoming a 'regulated autonomy' in which the work of teachers is increasingly monitored and policed. Such an approach fails to recognize the interpersonal nature of teaching and the extent to which it draws on personal resources and hence is experienced by teachers as both dehumanizing and deprofessionalizing (Ball,

2003). Concurrently, the increasing influence of international assessment regimes such as the OECD's PISA (Organisation for Co-operation and Economic Development Programme for International Student Assessment) on national policies and pedagogic prescriptions of international organizations and their technical experts overlook the contextualized nature of teachers' knowledge.

Managerial constructions of teacher professionalism are broadly evident in government policy, with Whitty (2008) indicating that the most powerful determinant of teacher professionalism today is the state, not the profession itself. Especially in the global South, state policy is strongly influenced by the reports and recommendations of international organizations (IOs) and foreign governments which act as donors and funders. IO approaches to teacher professionalism are not always explicitly stated but are evident in how teachers and their work are positioned within their commissioned research, reports and policy recommendations. The World Bank is a particularly influential donor. As noted earlier, the structural adjustment policies advocated by the World Bank and the International Monetary Fund (IMF) in the 1980s had severe consequences for teachers' pay and conditions of service. The Bank has also strongly supported the privatization of education by increasing marketization and through advocating policies such as performance by results, the use of contract teachers and the use of technology and learning resources made available by private contractors. As we will see, these policies have had a significant impact on the perceptions of teacher professionalism in countries such as India and Colombia.

Although the World Bank has a track record of research on teacher management, pay and conditions (for example, Mulkeen, 2005, 2010; Mulkeen et al, 2007), it is only in recent years that the Bank has engaged in global debates about the nature of teacher professionalism. The recent document entitled *Successful Teachers, Successful Students: Recruiting and Supporting Society's Most Crucial Profession* sets out the Bank's policy approach to teachers (Evans and Beteille, 2019). The approach, targeted at governments, equates teacher professionalism with teacher effectiveness, which, it is argued, contributes to education quality. In the discourses of the World Bank, education quality is correlated with the performance of learners in high-stakes assessments. Performance in these assessments is, in turn, equated with improvements in economic growth and productivity. This instrumental understanding of quality stands in contrast to the more expansive view of education quality proposed by UNESCO (above). Based on evidence from school effectiveness studies and practice in 'high-performing' countries such as Finland, Singapore and Shanghai (China), the World Bank offers five principles for improving teacher professionalism. These are set out in Box 3.2.

The attention to professionalizing teachers' employment and working conditions in some of the principles, including principle 1, accord with concerns of the teachers in our study.

Box 3.2: Five principles for improving teacher professionalism

Principle 1: Make teaching an attractive profession by improving its status, compensation policies and career progression structures.

Principle 2: Ensure pre-service education includes a strong practicum component to ensure teachers are well equipped to transition and perform effectively in the classroom.

Principle 3: Promote meritocratic selection of teachers, followed by a probationary period, to improve the quality of the teaching force.

Principle 4: Provide continuous support and motivation, in the form of high-quality in-service training and strong school leadership, to allow teachers to continually improve.

Principle 5: Use technology wisely to enhance the ability of teachers to reach every student, factoring in their areas of strength and development.

Source: Béteille and Evans (2021)

However, as principles targeted at policy makers, the top-down orientation fails to reflect contextual challenges teachers face in the global South or the more all-embracing view of professionalism proposed by teachers in the study.

A social justice approach to teacher professionalism

There is a relatively small but growing literature that relates teacher professionalism to ideas of social justice. Much of this literature critiques managerialist discourses such as those put forward by the World Bank (as noted earlier) for providing a narrow technocratic view of professionalism. It counterposes the view of the teacher as technocrat with the view of the teacher as a reflexive practitioner with agency and autonomy (for example, Govender et al, 2016). It can be seen as more closely aligned with and building on the rights-based approach outlined earlier. It is distinctive, however, in relating ideas of teacher professionalism to an insistence that education expands children's and young people's capacities and opportunities, including through dismantling conditions of oppression and exploitation. Within this literature, one influential framing of social justice is that offered by the capability approach of Amartya Sen and Martha Nussbaum (for example, Sen, 1999, 2011; Nussbaum, 2000, 2011; Robeyns, 2017). This frames social justice in terms of the capabilities (opportunity freedoms) available to individuals and groups to achieve functionings ('beings' and 'doings') that they have reason to value. Within the educational literature, the capability approach is often seen as a way of challenging the focus on a narrow range of skills associated with the human capital approach and instead focusing on a range of cognitive and affective outcomes of education that can support the development of valued capabilities and functions relevant for supporting sustainable livelihoods within peaceful and democratic societies (Walker and Unterhalter, 2007; Tikly and Barrett, 2011, 2013; Tikly, 2013).

A key concern within this literature is teaching for social justice. In keeping with Friere's ideas (for example, Friere, 1970; Darder, 2017), this includes raising learners' critical consciousness of the social forces that circumscribe their life opportunities. In the field of education and development, feminists and indigenous activists have been involved in critical decolonizing praxis (Aikman, 2011; Avalos, 2013). As we discuss later, such efforts have been evident at times in our countries of research focus, including the involvement of teachers in mass literacy campaigns linked to *Ujamaa* (African socialism) in Tanzania in the 1960s and 1970s (Buchert, 1994) and the role of Colombian teachers in the pedagogical movement (*Movimiento Pedagógico*) during the 1980s, which included a focus on promoting indigenous knowledge in the curriculum and resisted curricular reforms that teachers argued eroded their professionalism (Acevedo Terazona, 2013).

Social justice literature recognizes that educational institutions are themselves part of systems that reproduce oppression and exploitation, such as through selectively privileging children and young people from certain groups (for example, children from middle-class or white homes) while limiting the opportunities of others. Hence, teachers can and often are complicit in reproducing injustice. This includes violent behaviours, specifically teacher–on–student violence and student–on–teacher violence. The meting out of corporal punishment to learners is an ongoing concern, especially in low- and middle-income countries (UNICEF, 2015). Sexualized and gender-based violence is also widespread, where both teachers and students may be perpetrators (UNESCO, 2019). Violence, including gender-based violence, is an integral feature of postcolonial societies, both in countries at war and those at peace (Dunne et al, 2005; Parkes, 2015). In the global South, a key concern in the research literature is the effect of poor salaries and conditions of service on the ability of teachers to realize their professional identities (Avalos, 2013) and the inadequacy of teacher education programmes to assist teachers in developing their capabilities as educators (Tao, 2014).

Violence in education, however, is a problem of both the global North and the global South. At the time of writing, Western democracies are coming to terms with a long, dark history of systematic abuse of indigenous and vulnerable children within boarding schools (for example, Voce et al, 2021). In the UK, young people are calling attention to the prevalence of sexual harassment targeted at girls and violence towards LGBTQ+ students in secondary schools (for example, King-Hill, 2021). Literature applying social justice perspectives in post-conflict contexts provides a critically hopeful perspective on teachers' potential to build peace and social cohesion (Horner et al, 2015; Novelli and Sayed, 2016). Situating teachers as actors within complex local and national histories, this body of work argues for creating spaces where teachers can debate complex histories of conflict and oppression and reflect on how these continue to influence their professional identity (Novelli and Sayed, 2016; Paulson et al, 2020). As discussed in the following chapters, many of the perspectives of teachers in our study resonated with the themes identified by researchers working within a social justice approach. We also note that within this literature problems of teacher professionalism were most directly related to decolonizing education (Lavia, 2006; Walsh, 2015).

FOUR

Teacher Professionalism and the Coloniality of Power

Over the following three chapters, we draw on a decolonial framework to explore teachers' accounts of their professional lives. We use a framework developed by Ndlovu-Gatsheni (2013), who identifies three dimensions of coloniality: the coloniality of power, the coloniality of knowledge and the coloniality of being. Each is considered, in turn, as a way of framing the perspectives of the teachers involved in the study. Each dimension draws attention to different aspects of teacher professionalism. The first, coloniality of power, provides a means for understanding the emergence of mass education systems in the global South as a context for teacher professionalism; the second, coloniality of knowledge, provides a critical framework for considering the Eurocentric nature of the curriculum but also the predominance of Western ways of conceiving issues of curriculum and pedagogy and teacher professionalism itself. The third dimension, the coloniality of being, allows for a consideration of the everyday realities that impact the lived experiences of the teachers in the study.

The main arguments developed in this chapter are that global discourses do not consider the colonial and postcolonial legacies in how teacher professionalism is defined, understood and implemented. In this regard, and despite some similarities, teacher professionalism has developed under very different conditions in formerly colonized as compared to formerly colonizing countries. As will be further argued, however, it is important not to homogenize the colonial and postcolonial legacies in each country of research focus. Each has a different history of colonialism involving differing colonizing powers with diverse motives. European colonization of India and Colombia can be traced back to the late 15th century, while Rwanda and Tanzania were colonized as part of the European scramble for Africa from the late 19th century. Colombia recently celebrated its *bicentenario* of independence from Spanish rule. As in other Latin American countries, coloniality manifests in part through what is sometimes described as settler colonialism (for example, Castellanos, 2017) or a Latin American understanding of colonialism that implies settlement and 'creolization' that mingles with the legacies and realities of US imperialism (Speed, 2017). Ethiopia has never been colonized (although the Italians briefly occupied it). It has, nonetheless, been located, like formerly colonized African countries, at the periphery of the global economy and subject to relationships of economic and political dependency (Triulzi, 1982). Ethiopia, together with Rwanda and Tanzania, is a low-income, agrarian economy, whereas India and Colombia have more advanced service and manufacturing sectors and are classified as middle-income. As noted, India is also included as a 'rising power' or BRICS (Brazil, Russia, India, China and South Africa) economy. In political terms, all of the countries, except India, have gone through periods of autocratic rule, although all now describe themselves as multiparty democracies. Rwanda has emerged from a long period of protracted conflict between different interests within the state and civil society; a current peace process in Colombia seeks to end decades of armed conflict but is plagued by politicization and renewed violence, while high levels of communal violence currently characterize India. In the case of Ethiopia, Rwanda and India, conflict has often revolved around ethnic divisions that in the case of Rwanda and India can be traced back to colonial times.

It is also important to recognize differences and similarities in the nature of colonial and postcolonial education policies, as will be further elaborated later.[1] The introduction of Western-style education by colonizing powers occurred at different times and served differing motives. In Colombia, Western education was introduced under Spanish rule by missionaries in the 16th century mainly to cater for the children of the colonizers, while in India 'modern' education was introduced under the English in the early 19th century as a means to anglicize the children of indigenous elites and to create a cadre of graduates who could staff the colonial administration. Schooling was introduced in Rwanda and Tanzania once again predominantly by missionaries from the mid-19th century and then formalized at the beginning of the 20th century under German rule, also with the motive of producing skills to service the colonial bureaucracy and as a means to enculturate elites. Although Ethiopia has a long history of formal education within Christian and Islamic traditions, its first 'modern' schools date from the early 20th century. Modelled on European institutions, these schools were established primarily for the ruling elite to meet the needs of national administration and international diplomacy (Bahru, 2002).

It should be emphasized from the outset that it is not being claimed that a decolonial perspective is the only perspective through which teacher professionalism in the global South can be understood. Nonetheless, it is suggested that a decolonial perspective provides a powerful lens for better understanding how teacher professionalism in many formerly colonized, low- and middle-income countries may be conceived. Through shining the spotlight on the colonial and postcolonial legacies in education, it can be seen as providing an important basis for critiquing dominant agendas as well as augmenting insights generated particularly by the rights-based and social justice perspectives identified earlier – a point we return to in the conclusion (Chapter seven).

The coloniality of power and the development of modern education systems

The first dimension of coloniality proposed by Ndlovu-Gatsheni is that of the *coloniality of power*, which denotes the continued dominance in economic and political terms of Western powers over those of the global South (Gray and Murphy, 2013; Kahler, 2013; Mohan, 2013; Stephen, 2014).[2] The analysis builds on earlier critiques of neocolonialism (Nkrumah, 1966), of dependency (Frank, 1970; Amin, 1997) and of the 'new imperialism' (Harvey, 2003; Tikly, 2004) but also draws on insights from postcolonial scholarship and accords with recent analyses of the 'postcolonial condition' in Africa (for example, Tikly, 2020). It is also used to explore the ways in which indigenous elites have often been co-opted into the 'colonial matrix of power' (Mignolo and Walsh, 2018) since colonial times and continue to exercise this power over the rest of the indigenous population. Education has been an important institution for the exercise of the coloniality of power.

Space does not allow for a full account of the coloniality of power but the development of global capitalism and global markets is linked to the colonial past in which populations in colonizing countries along with European heritage populations in white settler colonies such as the US, Australia and Canada benefitted economically and politically from colonial economies and from the exploitation and enslavement of native populations (Amin, 1997; Hoogvelt, 1997). Based largely on extractive and exploitative production methods aimed at maximizing profit, the development of capitalism under colonialism led to the break-up of indigenous livelihoods and social structures, and often resulted in highly unequal and ethnically fragmented societies. It has also contributed to environmentally damaging practices, including the pollution of land, rivers and sea (Perry, 2020b, 2020a). Even after independence, as Nkrumah (1966) pointed out in his seminal account of neocolonialism, economic relationships between formerly colonized countries and those of the metropole continued to be based on the extraction of raw materials to support industrialization in the global North.

For Ndlovu-Gatsheni and other postcolonial and decolonial critics, the coloniality of power is reflected in the nature of the state in postcolonial societies. European colonialism resulted in the introduction of highly centralized and authoritarian state structures which were intended to serve the interests of the colonizers and did not acknowledge some of the complexities of incorporating into one territory diverse ethnic groups and in some instances the challenges involved in governing vast, sparsely populated swathes of land given limited governmental capacities (Herbst, 2000). Indigenous elites were assimilated into these existing structures. As Mamdani (1996) has cogently argued, this led to an increasing bifurcation between urban elites and rural dwellers and to the use of the state to advance the interests of some ethnic groups that had previously been favoured by the colonizers at the expense of others.

The mode of rule in postcolonial states has variously been described as 'personal rule', 'elite accommodation' and 'belly politics' and as a 'shadow' or 'neo-patrimonial state' (Boas and McNeill, 2004). In the model of the neo-patrimonial state, bureaucratic and patrimonial norms coexist. The state is able to extract and redistribute resources but this process, unlike in the Westphalian state model, is privatized.[3] 'In redressing the colonial legacy of racially inherited privilege, the independent states create a specific patrimonial path of re-distribution which divides the indigenous majority along regional, religious, ethnic and at times, family lines' (Boas and McNeill, 2004, p 33). In the context of the cold war, state building became implicated in global politics, with both Western and Eastern powers propping up sometimes corrupt and authoritarian regimes in support of their own global ambitions and economic interests. Access to state resources has also provided a source of conflict in many parts of the formerly colonized world, which, together with the effects of poverty and inequality, has fuelled increasing levels of South–South and South–North migration.

For example, in Colombia an armed conflict has been fought between Marxist-inspired guerrilla and state and para-state forces since the early 1960s. The roots of this confrontation can be traced to conflicts over the highly unequal distribution of wealth and political power in a country with a wide range of natural and human resources (for example, Bravo, 2015). Historically, teacher trade unionists have often been at the forefront of wider struggles for workers' rights and many teacher trade unionists have been targeted and killed by right-wing militias (Novelli, 2010). Conflict, economic crisis and poverty have also fuelled migration between neighbouring Venezuela and Colombia, leading recently to an influx of refugees into the Colombian education system, particularly in the region neighbouring the Venezuelan border, whereas earlier, in Colombia's armed conflict, Venezuela received Colombia refugees.

Data collection in Tigray, Ethiopia, took place against the backdrop of civil war between the national government in Addis Ababa and the regional government of Tigray, which began in November 2020. The full impact of this ongoing conflict remains unknown, but as of August 2021 included at least 2,805 well-documented civilian deaths, 400,000 people in famine conditions (Annys et al, 2021) and an estimated 5.2 million people in Tigray requiring humanitarian assistance (OCHA, 2021). Schools in Tigray closed at the start of the conflict (OCHA, 2021), and the teachers who participated in this study explained that the classrooms which had not been destroyed by fighting were being used either as military barracks or as temporary accommodation for internally displaced persons (IDPs). A more detailed case study of the war and its effects on teachers and their work is provided in a supplementary chapter at the end of the book (Chapter eight). As will be discussed, conflict has had a profound effect on teachers' work and well-being.

A major implication of neoliberal-inspired reform since the 1980s has been a convergence of development paths. Neoliberalism has also been associated with the 'hollowing out' (Ferguson, 2006) of the state. That is to say, whereas in the post-independence era states were seen as the main vehicles for various development projects and were often characterized by assertive indigenous leadership, this has been increasingly challenged under neoliberalism. Rather, cutbacks in government expenditure and the streamlining of state bureaucracies have had the perverse effect of increasing dependency as the capacity to govern has decreased further.

The coloniality of power is exemplified in the ability of Western powers to continue to exert control over key areas of global policy, including trade, development assistance and education, partly through the influence they exert in global governance agendas and over international organizations (Tikly, 2017; Jean, 2020). In the context of neoliberalism and conditional lending on the part of the World Bank and other donors from the early 1980s, global interests have often predominated over national ones through the mechanisms of conditional lending from multilateral organizations and bilateral aid in shaping national policy agendas (Ferguson, 2006). More recently, China and other rising powers have begun to exert ever greater soft power over areas such as education in pursuit of their own agendas (Gray and Murphy, 2013; Kahler, 2013; Mohan, 2013; Stephen, 2014). It is important here, however, to see the effects of neoliberal reform in a more global perspective as well. As discussed earlier, neoliberalism has also impacted the nature of the state and understandings of teacher professionalism in high-income contexts even if the effects have arguably been more overt in the global South (Govender et al, 2016).

The emergence of 'modern' education systems

It is against this backdrop of the coloniality of power that the emergence of modern education systems in each country needs to be understood. Key characteristics of modern education systems can be traced back to their introduction under colonialism. Colonial education was complicit in the wider colonial project by rendering the colonized 'economically useful and politically docile' (Rodney, 1973, p 71). It was an important vehicle for processes of elite formation (although this had contradictory implications in the context of struggles for national liberation as these were often led by Western-educated indigenous elites). Colonial education systems were highly unequal, with limited access to primary education and even more restricted access to later stages of education.

Immediately following independence in African countries and India (where nationalist leaders had made several attempts to universalize basic education under the British government), there were efforts to introduce mass state education in support of national development visions. In Tanzania, for instance, in a massive nationwide effort, a rapidly trained cadre of young teachers, most with little more than primary education themselves, were posted around the country, where they were charged with mobilizing communities to build schools. Alongside this expansion of primary education, an adult literacy programme was also rolled out, often facilitated by teachers after school hours. By 1981, Tanzania claimed it had achieved universal primary education and that adult literacy rates, which were barely 8 per cent in 1962, had reached 80 per cent (Buchert, 2002). In Colombia, as elsewhere in Latin America, education expanded unevenly after independence in the 1800s, at times driven by religious, state and other actors and interests. Education expanded to reach most students in the last century, in line with international and regional initiatives like Education for All and government commitments, and became Latin America's most educated nation under former President Manuel Santos.

Despite efforts to universalize education in the post-independence era, many state education systems remain chronically under-resourced and highly unequal in terms of access along lines of socio-economic disadvantage, gender, ethnicity and locality. Rwanda and Ethiopia are yet to achieve universal primary education and access to secondary and tertiary education remains even more restricted. Assessment systems introduced under colonialism continue to act primarily as a filter mechanism to limit access to secondary and tertiary education.

It is also from the colonial era that many of the other characteristics of modern education systems can ultimately be traced (Altbach and Kelly, 1978; Pritchett, 2013; Tikly, 2020). For example, and despite more recent efforts to decentralize, key aspects of education policy remain highly centralized – a point that is taken up later in relation to a discussion of the curriculum. In Colombia, there is no national curriculum and decision making over teaching content rests with schools, teachers and local education authorities, though, as will be seen, teachers continue to critique centralized control over education and the undue influence of national and international testing regimes in restricting curricular autonomy. Another feature of colonial education systems is that they were highly bureaucratic in nature. In the postcolonial era newly independent states sought to mimic the bureaucratic and centralized nature of 'modern' (that is, Western industrialized) states (Pritchett, 2013). In their day-to-day lives, teachers are expected to spend many hours on administrative work. A teacher in India shared the multiple roles that teachers are supposed to perform in school. This can divert time from teaching, leaving students unattended. Teachers are often made to feel that non-teaching administrative work is far more important. Teaching suffers and teachers can feel frustrated and helpless.

> 'Sometimes during a regular day at school as a teacher I lose stream of the teaching–learning process due to the administrative duties that I am expected to attend to on priority, like the distribution of books, opening of bank accounts for children, issuing of Aadhar card for new

admissions, disbursal of scholarship money for minority children.' (FGD, Indian primary school teacher)

The bureaucratic nature of education systems also has implications for teachers' pay. On the one hand, the majority of teachers in the countries of research focus have historically been employed in the post-independence era as civil servants, which provides, in however limited a form, a basic level of pay and job security. This stands in contrast to teachers in the private sector, who are often employed on short-term, insecure contracts and at lower rates of pay (Ashley et al, 2014). On the other hand, the basic inefficiency of bureaucratic systems, exacerbated by issues such as COVID-19 and the onset of conflict, means that, as our data reveal, in some contexts, such as Ethiopia and India, teachers are not paid regularly, and in some instances not at all (see also Cameron, 2021). As one teacher in India explained:

'Teachers in municipal government schools do not get paid on time and there is a pay lag of four to five months. The government needs to act on this immediately and release teachers' pending salary, especially challenging during the time of the pandemic.' (FGD, Indian primary school teacher)

Closely linked to their bureaucratic nature, education systems have since colonial times been top-down in nature, reflecting wider patterns of colonial and postcolonial governance. One aspect of this is that teachers' unions and professional associations have had limited voice in educational reform. The lack of teacher voice in key areas of policy and practice was remarked on by the teachers. As one teacher in Tanzania explained, "[e]ducation policy [in] Tanzania is not inclusive as teachers are not involved in decision making matters [and] do not have autonomy in matters pertaining to the teaching profession". According to the teachers who participated in focus group discussions in Rwanda, the education policy changes tend to be abrupt and top-down. Teachers reported that adjusting to policy changes is difficult because they have had no voice in the process of policy design, but it also affects the ability of governments to properly implement policy. One Rwandan teacher argued that every "education policy [that] is aimed at improving learning ... should bear in mind what happens at the classroom level and ... teachers need to have a voice in the policy making process so that the policy captures practical realities at the classroom level" (FGD, Rwandan primary school teacher). Teachers in India argued that there needs to be a feedback system through which teachers' voices about issues of curriculum, pedagogy and other professional concerns are heard, so that the process is not so top-down.

Teachers across all contexts commented on the importance but also the difficulties of organizing effectively within trade unions so as to have their voices heard. Historically, teacher trade unions have played a prominent role in anticolonial struggles. However, in the post-independence era, in countries such as Tanzania, they have often found it difficult to maintain their autonomy, effectiveness and sense of relevance for teachers (Nchimbi, 2018). As the teachers in Rwanda lamented, there is a lack of a strong and collective platform where their voices can be heard. About half of the teachers interviewed stated that they did not even know teachers' unions and professional associations existed, while others questioned their effectiveness, reflecting concerns in the wider literature (Cameron, 2020). The teachers in Colombia were, however, largely critical of the current role of the teachers' union federation (FECODE) in defending the rights of teachers, especially in rural areas, and in failing to work with teachers collaboratively on pedagogical issues or to engage with the government on pressing issues concerning the quality of education. This must be seen in historical context, as FECODE has in the past contributed to the promotion of important changes in educational policies through its leading role in the *Movimiento Pedagógico en Colombia*

(Pedagogical Movement of Colombia), which resisted top-down policy changes to curricula and teaching standards (Peñuela Contreras and Rodríguez Murcia, 2006; Acevedo Terazona, 2013).

Global agendas and national education policy

Teachers' work has been profoundly impacted by global agendas advocated by donors and supported by national governments. From the 1980s onwards, the neocolonial influence of Western powers was exercised through aid and loan conditionalities foisted on indebted governments. These unleashed structural adjustment policies, which integrated low- and middle-income nations into a globalizing economy on unfavourable terms (Tikly, 2004) and prevented expansion of basic education, so that enrolment ratios declined. By the early 21st century, various national governments had in place a remarkably similar policy architecture consisting in a national development vision, sector development plans and strategies readily intelligible to aid agencies and external consultants. Through these the MDG agenda could be cascaded into national development policies.

Teachers' work has been profoundly impacted by global agendas advocated by donors and supported by national governments (for example, Crossley et al, 2017). The MDGs, for instance, prioritized basic education expansion. The relative success of the MDGs is reflected in the increase in class sizes noted by many teachers, which has often occurred at the expense of education quality (Tikly and Barrett, 2013). The SDGs can be seen as placing greater emphasis on the development of all subsectors of education and training, including teacher training, and focusing on the quality of education. At the same time, however, SDG4 has extended the basic education cycle to lower secondary education, perpetuating the relentless pressure of expansion with its attendant challenges for quality and teacher supply (UIS, 2006, 2012; Lewin, 2007; UNESCO, 2014). More recent trends in global policy have also profoundly affected teachers' work, as the perspectives of teachers cited suggest. Of particular relevance for the teachers in this study are the move towards competency-based curricula, emphasis on outcome-based education and the introduction of educational technologies, which accelerated during the COVID-19 pandemic.

Overcrowded, heterogeneous classes

One implication of the rapid expansion of primary and lower secondary education is that teachers face challenging, dynamic classrooms. Since the 1990 Jomtien conference, international focus has been on ensuring that all children can access primary schooling, with calls for free, universal primary education implemented with the MDGs in 2000. Across the world, the population of out-of-school children had fallen from 376.1 million in 2000 to an estimated 258.4 million in 2019 before the onset of the COVID-19 pandemic (UNESCO/ UIS, 2019). Increased student populations have had serious implications across all dimensions of teachers' work in the global South. In Ethiopia, for example, the primary sector grew from accommodating 3 million students in the 1990s to more than 21 million students today, and the student–teacher ratio has more than doubled over this period. As in many similar contexts, education has shifted from catering only to a small, comparatively advantaged section of the population to a near-universal one. Parents, as Colombian teachers noted, may not have been educated themselves or may not see the relevance of schooling, especially when it appears unaligned with the jobs marketplace. Often, formal education cannot compete with informal and sometimes illegal work opportunities.

Overcrowded classrooms are a common theme across several of the case contexts, a strain on both the existing school infrastructure and the (often) sole teacher responsible. In Tanzania, in urban areas where drop-out rates are lower, teachers reported classrooms having up to 180 students within a class: one primary school teacher noted that "teachers are able to deal with students who sit in front of the class only. It is very hard for a teacher to pass up to the back to see students". Policy stipulates that secondary class sizes are to be capped at 40 pupils, but a shortage of classrooms means that classes of up to 80 are common (Ministry of Education and Vocational Training, 2018; Kasuga, 2019). According to one Ethiopian teacher, "Imagine a teacher that teaches five to six classes, each with sixty students. I don't think the teacher will make sound evaluations. After all, he may not know who is progressing and who is not." In India, where teacher–student ratios can reach 1:65, the challenge of tracking large student groups was exacerbated during the pandemic, when so many students lacked digital connectivity. Large class sizes hindered teachers in providing quality education and fuelled fatigue, burnout and even boredom.

This is in a context where teachers also struggle to accommodate the diverse needs of their heterogeneous student groups. In both India and Tanzania, teachers commented on the challenge of balancing the different religious and cultural backgrounds of students (and their parents) within one class group. In Colombia, where the education system has had to accommodate a large influx of Venezuelan refugee children (UNESCO, 2020), teachers often take on roles as counsellors and social workers, providing children with food, supplies and study guides. Many of those students, due to the conditions of their migration, are behind in the expected learning for their grade level. In distant rural areas, multi-grade classrooms are common. Teachers across the other contexts also reported having multiple levels of preparedness for the grade and subject in one class group: in Ethiopia, for example, a policy of automatic promotion means that one classroom may contain students with a variety of learning levels that teachers must work to accommodate and teach. In Tanzania, teachers reported the increasing vulnerability of girls due to the distances they have to travel to get to school. A woman teacher working

The privatization of education

A key aspect of structural adjustment lending during the 1980s, as noted, was efforts to reduce state expenditure on education, including teachers' salaries and pensions. Government expenditure has been affected by austerity measures in the wake of the 2008 global financial crash and has not kept pace with educational expansion or the more recent shift in emphasis on the quality of education. Recent levelling off of aid for education has exacerbated the financial crisis (UNESCO, 2015). In this context, the World Bank has consistently advocated for increased privatization of education. Privatization can be understood as comprising two interrelated elements, both of which are linked to the spread of neoliberal-inspired policies in education since the 1980s (Ball and Youdell, 2008; Verger et al, 2016).

The first is exogenous privatization, which involves the opening up of public education services to private sector participation, including on a profit-making basis, such that the private sector is invited to design, manage or deliver aspects of education. Private schools have long been a feature of the educational landscape in each of the five countries of research focus, catering predominantly for the children of the elite. In each of the countries of research focus, there has also been a rapid growth in the numbers of for-profit low fee private schools (LFPS), and indeed resistance to privatization was a key aim of Colombia's *Movimiento Pedagógico* (Peñuela Contreras and Rodríguez Murcia, 2006). Many are run by international chains. A key feature of many of these schools is that teachers are often employed on temporary contracts and at lower rates of pay than teachers who are employed as civil servants (Verger et al, 2016). For example, India's *New*

Education Policy (GoI, 1986), embedded during the early phase of liberalization, succeeded in institutionalizing educational inequities by opening pathways for differentiated curricula and schooling systems. Since the early 1990s a series of systemic changes were instituted in the provisioning and practice of school and teacher education. Neoliberal reforms led to the withdrawal of state investment in pre-service teacher education and divested teachers of agency, while reducing curricula to minimum levels of learning, relegating teaching to lower-order cognitive skills and putting the onus of learning on the child. The bulk hiring of para-teachers and the neglect of developing institutional capacity to enhance teacher professionalism and deal with acute teacher shortages made way for private players to take over the educational space. Currently, over 95 per cent of teacher education institutions are in private hands.

A further form of exogenous privatization is the outsourcing of aspects of education, including the production of materials for use in public schools. The second, related form is endogenous privatization. This involves changes in the very nature and culture of education systems themselves through seeking to import techniques and practices from the private sector in order to make the use of public resources more effective and efficient. It might take many forms, among them the introduction of performance management techniques including the increasing use of contract teachers and payment by results.

Both of these forms of privatization impacted on the experiences of the teachers in the study. For example, in India teachers reported instances where colleagues on short-term contracts were laid off. Similarly, in Colombia teachers often lack permanent status, especially in some public schools which are under private administration, where contracts have a fixed term, and this also has an impact on their social benefits such as health insurance. In Ethiopia, the respondents reported that they knew of many teachers in private schools who had been laid off and had subsequently lost their livelihoods as a result of the ongoing conflict. As one teacher put it during a focus group discussion: "A number of teachers, especially those teachers that were working in the private schools did not get their salary since the beginning of the war in Ethiopia's Tigray regional state. Some teachers become homeless while others migrate to other cities and countries" (FGD, Ethiopian primary school teacher).

Teachers in Ethiopia and in Tanzania also commented on the effects of the increasing use of performance management techniques. In Ethiopia they reported that teacher evaluation is emphasized in policy but poorly implemented in practice and that they were subject to bias, with superiors awarding high scores to teachers that are obedient to their orders and low scores to those who challenge the authorities. "The scores of the performance appraisal don't represent the performance of teachers. Sadly, you may find teachers who cannot teach the subject appropriately but scored high in the performance appraisal results" (FGD, Ethiopian secondary school teacher).

Students also provide an evaluation of their teachers, which the respondents saw as a highly subjective, biased measure. Students were seen as giving higher scores to teachers who are less strict in taking attendance, in teaching subject lessons and in shaping the behaviour of students. In Tanzania, the introduction of Quality Assurance (QA) was supposed to be more supportive than the previous top-down and authoritarian system of school inspectors. However, this was not a view shared by the teachers interviewed or indeed by the key informants. As one informant put it: "In terms of the quality assurance system, of course there is an idea of moving from school inspection to quality assurance in the sense that instead of inspecting they discuss together. But ... nothing has been ... it is like inspection has been given another name" (Key informant, Tanzania).

In India, the teachers reported that the practice and culture of regular monitoring by school inspectors increased during the pandemic. Many teachers feel that whatever little autonomy they had in their physical classrooms pre-pandemic has been taken away completely. What to teach, how to teach, what to speak in the classroom, and how to speak in the classroom have become matters of grave concern, and several teachers felt that they were being watched all the time. The entire focus, according to the teachers, is on maintaining surveillance and on compiling data in terms of student attendance and participation, and submission of homework on WhatsApp groups. Every week teachers are expected to collate data on "how many students attended online classes, how many responded, how many did not respond". This led one teacher to comment:

> 'I am always pulled away from my primary duty as a teacher and directed towards other tasks which find their priority over teaching because of pressure from higher authorities … it is a kind of chain reaction. I often ask myself, have I also become the part of this chain?' (FGD, Indian primary school teacher)

Another teacher went on to add: "Sometimes I ask myself – is it even a school? and I a teacher anymore? Or is it just a building with multiple uses and I am a government employee assigned to do whatever work the authorities deem fit" (FGD, Indian primary school teacher).

FIVE

Teacher Professionalism and the Coloniality of Knowledge

The second dimension of Ndlovu-Gatsheni's understanding of coloniality, namely the *coloniality of knowledge*, is intimately entwined with the coloniality of power and refers to the predominance of Eurocentric epistemologies and conceptions of the world (see also Santos, 2012). This includes the way development is itself conceived, predominantly in Western capitalist terms, as a linear process of moving from largely agrarian economies reliant on the export of primary commodities to post-industrial societies characterized by a 'knowledge economy'. Education is conceived from this perspective as primarily contributing to the development of human capital. From a decolonial perspective, these ideas of development are problematic in that they often assume high-income economies to be the benchmark towards which other countries must strive. They also ignore other ideas about development and progress, including those rooted in non-Western knowledge and belief systems about the nature of social reality and human subjectivity and the relationship between human beings and the natural world. Further, through equating development with economic growth, they elide the consequences of untrammelled growth for environmental sustainability (Cortez Ochoa et al, 2021). In the postcolonial context, the coloniality of knowledge is also reflected in the centralized nature of curricula and the lack of emphasis placed on local knowledge and contexts by curriculum planners and teacher training institutions, with implications for teachers' agency.

Decontextualized and irrelevant curricula

Colonial education was instrumental in embedding a Western *episteme* (base of knowledge) as the basis for projecting Western views of modernity. Colonial curricula and textbooks promoted Western knowledge. In this way it contributed to the marginalization of indigenous religions, cultures and languages (Thiong'o, 1986) and led to a split between educated, often urban elites who had access to Western education and the majority, predominantly rural population. Schooling under colonialism also reflected wider inequalities, with opportunities to access education stratified along class, racial, ethnic and gender lines.

In some countries, such as Tanzania, there was an effort by post-independence governments to address the colonial legacy in education. In Tanzania in 1964, for example, Nyerere made universal primary education a central goal for his African socialist policies. Nyerere envisioned an education that would support 'mental decolonisation' and prepare young people for productive livelihoods within their home communities (Nyerere, 1967). Education for Self-Reliance was introduced into the curriculum, intended to create space for local elders to share their skills and knowledge (Buchert, 1994, p 110). In general, however, and despite efforts in some countries to contextualize curricula and pedagogical practices and to align educational purposes with post-independence development goals, curricula often remain detached from local contexts and realities of the learners and their communities, as many of the teachers in the study explained. Post-independence India, for example, adopted a 'modern education system' that was rooted in the colonial view of knowledge and of the Indian people. This system of education carried with it a constituted coloniality in which the hierarchical and hegemonic character of Brahmanical power remained central. The colonial epistemic frame was left uncontested despite initial postcolonial attempts to link quality education with indigenous views of education, and anticolonial and anti-caste discourses prevalent in the previous era of struggle against colonialism (Batra, 2020).

As part of global reform agendas, many countries have been encouraged to move towards more competency- and outcomes-based curricula so as to make them more relevant for development. In Tanzania, for instance, efforts have been made to vocationalize curricula, and vocational skills is now a compulsory subject at primary and secondary level. However, primary school teachers claimed that the *stadi za kazi* (vocational skills) curriculum is not relevant to the environment of their schools and that teachers should be afforded greater latitude in adapting the curriculum to local needs through integrating skills such as entrepreneurship, fishing and agriculture.

Subject-based curricula, patterned on those in the West with a hierarchy between theoretical/academic and vocational/applied knowledge, are still not adapted to enduring challenges of under-resourced education systems. There is often a failure to adapt school curricula to material constraints and at the same time draw on and engage with indigenous knowledge. As an Ethiopian teacher explained in relation to the new emphasis on teaching science, technology, engineering and mathematics (STEM) in secondary schools:

'If we need to develop our students in science and mathematics, future support should focus on the development of school laboratories. Our students are not exposed to science as needed. We told our students about the "pop" sound of a hydrogen and then students reiterate it. They do not know and identify which one is cation and which is an anion.' (FGD, Ethiopian secondary school teacher)

Echoing these sentiments, a secondary teacher of science in Tanzania stated that: "Poor laboratory equipment to support students' learning; students end up in studying theory only" (FGD, Tanzanian secondary school teacher).

In Colombia, teachers in this study argued for a move away from what they perceived as an overly instrumental curriculum and to make it more student oriented. They favoured greater attention to arts and culture in the curriculum, which are seen as fundamental elements for students' personal growth. They also suggested that there should be more emphasis on promoting gender awareness and environmental education. In the context of peacebuilding, the teachers argued the need for the curriculum to promote cultural changes that favour ethics and honesty, while discouraging the values associated with drug trafficking and violent conflict. Teachers proposed that students should be taught to be critical citizens in democracy.

The perceived lack of relevance of the curriculum is related by the teachers to its highly centralized/standardized nature, which is seen as limiting their ability to adapt curricula to the local needs. As one Tanzanian educator noted:

'[The] curriculum was centralized by assuming that all Tanzania should learn the same contents across the country. But in fact we need to think about it in another way, the curriculum needs to be decentralized as we have 26 regions with more than 122 ethnic groups. We need to give power to teachers on curriculum development and implementation so that they can include some issues from their local areas to be included in the curriculum.' (FGD, Tanzanian secondary school teacher)

Similarly, teachers in Colombia argued strongly against standardization of curricula, which do not respond to the different regional contexts, including the needs of indigenous, Afro-Colombian and other communities. The majority mentioned the need to contextualize subject guides. One teacher, referring to the guides, asked himself the question: "Where did they write this?" Teachers in India argued that even well-intentioned interventions by the government, such as the 'Happiness Curriculum' are overcentralized. According to the teachers, school inspectors tend to force teachers to follow the manual for the 'Happiness Curriculum', when in fact it is meant to be merely recommendatory. This makes the entire exercise mechanical and ineffective in achieving the desired objectives.

The perceived standardization and decontextualization of curricula was also linked by the teachers to the effects of high-stakes assessment regimes. In the context of highly unequal education systems, examinations have acted predominantly as a filtering mechanism limiting access to secondary and higher education and training. In India and Colombia, teachers commented on the role of international assessment regimes such as Programme for International Student Assessment (PISA) and Trends In International Mathematics and Science Study (TIMMS) in further entrenching standardization and limiting teacher autonomy. For the teachers in all of the countries, the phenomenon of 'teaching to the test' limited their ability to respond to the increasingly diverse needs of learners.

In some instances, the centralized nature of the curriculum and its lack of pedagogical relevance was exacerbated by the pandemic. In India, for example, as teaching shifted to online modes because of school shutdowns during the pandemic, several of the teachers had been given ready-made curricular and pedagogic content in the form of videos and worksheets to be disseminated to students. Teaching content is prepared by non-governmental and corporate organizations and imposed on teachers. The worksheets are often rigid and do not match up to any principles of teaching practices or learning. Giving an example of a language worksheet, one of the respondents said that activities are often based on a 'product' approach with a focus on 'grammar'. This approach does not help children develop reading comprehension capacity and skills. The process has become rigidly top-down with virtually no role for the teacher. Teachers have become mere conduits of 'information' in the form of worksheets and lessons.

> 'It has been almost ten days and I am yet to spend extended time with the children. Children were tired of asking that when are we going to study. I had no replies. All I had were registers, lists, more lists, cleanliness, children's bank accounts and several other registers, lists to be managed. I am perceived as a multitasker, a task-performer, a facilitator who has an expertise in both teaching and non-teaching tasks; a hygiene inspector for children; a person responsible for imbibing moral values in children. I am basically seen as an "Ashta bhujaaen" [eight-arms], more functional than anyone else.' (FGD, Indian primary school teacher)

Pedagogic communication has often taken the form of following 'orders' from the administration. Even when teachers feel that the worksheets are not pedagogically appropriate for students in their class, they do not have the space or any platform to raise doubts, objections and the need to discuss. For instance, the State Directorate of Education sent a circular making it mandatory for teachers of grade I to take 'dictation' twice a day in a separate notebook. Many teachers felt that such an activity is pedagogically inappropriate, but they had no means of making themselves heard. Teacher performance is assessed on the basis of 'complying' with these orders, so they are coerced into following them. Respondents said it was relatively easier to negotiate such impositions during pre-pandemic times. With the site of teaching shifting to online modes, even the little space they had to assert their autonomy and professional judgement has disappeared.

Global versus local languages

Colonial education often took place in the language of the colonizer, particularly at more senior levels. In all of the countries of research focus, with the exception of Ethiopia, the medium of instruction is in a global language. As the participating teachers from Rwanda explained, this poses significant challenges for teaching and learning, particularly for socio-economically disadvantaged learners in rural areas. In Rwanda, the language of instruction is a particular barrier for students and teachers alike (Pearson, 2013; Tolon, 2014; Cameron, 2020). English, instituted as the medium of instruction with the rapid 2009 shift, is still not widely spoken in Rwanda, where a vast majority speak one local language, Kinyarwanda. Teachers commented on seeing the gap between ambitious policy and what was possible in the context:

> 'Sometimes, we give children a zero or low mark well knowing that they could have succeeded if the exam was set in their mother tongue – a language they understand most – especially at lower primary. As a teacher, I feel painful when I see children failing because they do not understand English well knowing they have not had exposure to this new language in their communities.' (FGD, Rwandan primary school teacher)

Similarly, in Tanzania there are 123 ethnic groups and tribal languages spoken. Kiswahili is the language of instruction in pre-primary and primary education, while English is the language of instruction in lower and upper secondary schools. The use of English as a language of instruction is a challenge to many secondary schools, but there is currently poor support for students to transition to English-medium instruction (Ministry of Education and Vocational Training, 2018). It is worth pointing out that while academic and professional tertiary education normally uses English as the language of instruction, many graduates from lower secondary school will continue on to Kiswahili-medium vocational education and training.

So impracticable is the use of a language that many learners rarely hear outside of school that teachers across sub-Saharan

Africa have for decades improvised bilingual strategies (Clegg and Afitska, 2011; Benson, 2014; Clegg and Simpson, 2016). In Tanzania, teacher educators have worked collectively to develop a language supportive pedagogy (Erling et al, 2021), while in South Africa researchers have been exploring the potential of translanguaging as pedagogy (Probyn, 2015). Both these approaches allow students to use languages they know well in the classroom and hence to articulate knowledge from their community and home. They also exemplify the capacity of the teaching profession to generate pedagogic solutions to the dilemmas and contradictions posed by coloniality.

The digitization of teaching and learning

As noted in previous sections, the use of digital technologies has been increasingly identified by organizations such as the World Bank as a means for improving the quality of teaching and learning. There has been significant attention paid to the benefits of '21st century learning' for the global South over the past decade while the use of digital technologies to promote learning burgeoned during the COVID-19 pandemic. For example, Ethiopian teachers commented positively on how, prior to the conflict, support for STEM subjects had been increasing, including the use of plasma TV as a teaching aid. Social media (for example, Telegram) was also used to share documents and information with students during COVID-related school closures.

'The integration of the Plasma TV was so interesting to the profession. At least, you benefited from other experts and, at the same time, you know how other students (that is, those in other schools) are learning. So, it was becoming a platform to equate differences among teachers and schools. A student, irrespective of his location and kind of teacher assigned to teach him, had an optimum similarity in terms of the contents he was taught through the Plasma TV.' (FGD, Ethiopian secondary school teacher)

Teachers in Colombia stated that despite the precariousness of connectivity and the multiple problems that have arisen in getting students to access online platforms, online learning offers new opportunities for learning and is most likely here to stay after the pandemic.

Nonetheless, teachers expressed concerns about the digitization of learning in relation to their professionalism. First, teachers are seeing growing inequalities and reversals in access to schooling as a hard digital divide excludes children in rural areas and from poorer households in urban areas from accessing education (Dixon, 2019). This reflects evidence from the wider literature. For example, around three-quarters of rural primary schools in sub-Saharan Africa do not have access to electricity (UNESCO, 2017). A recent study found that of 450 million children in Africa, only around 19 million (4.2 per cent) are users of EdTech — for the most part, educational TV programmes (Crawfurd and Hares, 2020). The Ethiopian teachers pointed out the limited availability of EdTech generally in Ethiopian schools but particularly in rural areas. In India, children of migrant labourers who returned to villages cannot afford mobile phones. In Rwanda, teachers reported growing inequality in the quality of education between wealthier pupils enrolled in private schools and those served by the public sector. In Tanzania, one teacher stated that "ICT [information and communications technology] is almost impossible in some places in Tanzania because there is a lack of source of power, especially in rural areas. ICT use in teaching can be possible only in urban schools but most of Tanzanian residents are living in rural areas" (FGD, Tanzanian secondary school teacher).

A related concern is the lack of access to ICT facing many teachers. Teachers in Rwanda and Ethiopia reported that they cannot afford laptops: "teachers don't have computers to write exams" (FGD, Rwandan primary school teacher). The move to online learning also raised concerns among some teachers about their changing relationships with learners. This prompted one teacher in Colombia to ask: "How can we maintain the bonds with our students in the virtual world?" One of the roles of teachers is to sustain bonds of affection. School is often the place where students can express what may be affecting them, such as domestic violence, drug use or teenage pregnancy.

In India, the teachers expressed fears that the increased digitization of learning during the pandemic was also associated with new forms of surveillance. For example, the head of the school and even the school inspector are part of the WhatsApp groups that teachers create with students. These are monitored and checked by administrative officers during inspections too. Any talk about the administration and the school is seen as conspiring against them. Technology has provided the opportunity to record whatever is happening at a given moment and send it as a complaint. Respondents shared that often colleagues record videos of each other if there is a debate or conflict between them and register that as a complaint. These are frequently one-sided narratives which harm the collegiality and spirit of working in collaboration. Further, teachers fear that this surveillance system will continue beyond the pandemic via methods such as CCTV cameras to monitor teachers in real time. The culture of surveillance will most certainly stand in the way of teachers trying to understand their students' lived experiences, on-the-ground realities and discussing real issues with them. This means that education will become increasingly disconnected from their immediate social and personal milieu. That will make the job of teaching extremely difficult and teachers will also be overly conscious of how they 'should' behave in school and in classrooms. "We will not be able to be spontaneous in class, or even relate to our students with the closeness required for establishing a bond with our learners. We are also worried that the relationship between teachers and students will change even more" (FGD, Indian primary school teacher).

Teachers in India also feared being 'replaced' by apps and other technology. In the coming years, teachers will no longer be living, thinking beings; they will become mere tools in the hands of the administration. This is already visible in advertisements of companies that offer all kinds of educational technology devices, digitized content and accessories. One EdTech application (Byju) portrays teachers' roles to be replaceable by a tech app. Aggressive advertisement campaigns by EdTech companies have convinced parents that apps are necessary for children to succeed. Many parents even believe that subscription to these is compulsory. In years to come, the hold of the market will be tighter in terms of dictating school curricula and pedagogic approaches. The aggressive push for technology and artificial intelligence in policy, together with market forces, will reduce teachers' agency even further.

Teachers in all contexts explained that, in the absence of proper training, they have often struggled to teach themselves how to connect and manage virtual platforms. They have had to acquire the technological equipment themselves and pay the costs of data plans to ensure connectivity. Research on digital inequalities and specifically digital literacy inequalities have shown that there are deeper divides and inequalities that move beyond discussions about access and connectivity, from a have/have-not debate to a more pressing can/cannot debate (Morrell and Rowsell, 2019). That is, lack of access and connectivity are leaving parts of the world behind due to a lack of virtual platforms and the latest technologies, but are also limiting severely the understandings and skills that children and young people can have and can achieve because they cannot engage properly and meaningfully in virtual environments. The tremendous digital inequalities faced by the global South have been referred to as black holes (Castells, 2000), contexts where people make things work and learn 'on the fly' in the face of scant Wi-Fi, patchy connectivity and primitive technologies.

The inadequacy and lack of relevance of teacher education

Initial teacher education in many low- and middle-income contexts has also been affected by the coloniality of knowledge. That is to say, it has often been didactic in orientation and divorced from the realities of the classroom. Teacher training curricula have often lagged behind changes to school curricula, policy and practice (Moon, 2012; Pryor et al, 2012; Westbrook et al, 2013; Batra, 2014). Many of the teachers spoke of their dissatisfaction with the lack of relevance of initial teacher education in preparing teachers for the classroom. According to one Tanzanian teacher educator, for example:

> 'The challenge with student teachers is that we impart them with irrelevant knowledge that cannot help them to have self-employment. The assessment mode we use focuses much on measuring their mastering of the material we deliver to them; theoretically they do not possess any skill that they can use in practice and real life.' (Key informant, Tanzania)

The Colombian teachers interviewed argued that "there is a broken bridge between them and the schools, as teachers do not have experience in the classroom before arriving at the schools. There are no real internships in the undergraduate programmes" (FGD, Colombian secondary school teacher).

There was also criticism of the perceived lack of relevance of curricula. One educator in Colombia argued, for instance, that attention should be given to the 'whole' role of the teacher, not just the teacher as an academic expert. Education must contribute to eradicating child abuse as well as sexual and work-related exploitation, and to achieving safe conditions for children and adolescents. In Ethiopia and India, the teachers interviewed suggested that greater emphasis should be placed on how to make use of digital resources, while in Rwanda the teachers talked about the need to prepare teachers to teach in English.

In India, where the bulk of initial teacher education programmes are now privately delivered and state investment in the sector is likely to see a further decline, teachers expressed fear that teacher education will morph into a factory model where the expectation would be to produce 'trained teachers' with the least amount of resource investment. Instead of focusing on real education and critical thinking, priorities would shift to enhancing market-based skills among schoolteachers. The base of students aspiring to teacher education programmes is likely to see a major shift, with a steep decline in the representation of marginalized groups.

The teachers across all contexts expressed their desire to undertake continuing professional development (CPD). Teachers also welcomed opportunities to get involved in in-service training and seminars to develop themselves professionally. In India, some of the respondents said they are part of Delhi University's Central Institute of Education Literacy Group, which is a support group for language teachers where they can exchange views on teaching practices and discuss specific issues. Teachers miss these discussions as all such interactions came to a halt during the pandemic. Some lamented the closure of the Regional Resource Centre for Elementary Education in CIE that offered various platforms for teachers to organize study sessions and undertake classroom-based research with mentoring support. In Colombia, two teachers spoke about their experience as beneficiaries of public training programmes. One of them is involved in the *Todos a aprender* (Let's All Learn) initiative, which is recognized by UNESCO and has been successful in regions such as Magdalena, particularly in the Sierra Nevada de Santa Marta. The programme provides scholarships for master's degrees, fully paid for with public resources, and even the possibility of going on to a doctorate.

However, a key concern flagged by many of the teachers that is also reflected in the wider literature is the lack of opportunities to undertake relevant continuing professional development (Moon, 2012; Westbrook et al, 2013; Komba and Mwakabenga, 2020). As one Tanzanian teacher explained: "There are many changes taking place in the curriculum but teachers are not prepared to accommodate those changes. There is need to conduct thorough research to accommodate changes of curriculum and teachers need to be trained to accommodate those change" (FGD, Tanzanian primary school teacher).

In Rwanda, teachers expressed the need for CPD to assist them in coping with top-down changes such as in the language of instruction policy. They lamented a clear policy concerning CPD and the lack of incentives for teachers to enrol in CPD programmes. In Ethiopia, teachers reported that CPD programmes in areas such as STEM education, while welcome, are often too short and lack a practical component.

'Summer training is too short. Especially, for sciences fields such as mathematics, physics and chemistry, it is not only short but impossible to cover some basic contents of the subject. You never go to the lab to test and see how things work. You never exercise and read additional books to develop your understanding. What you do is only reading teacher notes given either in modules or power point slides and pass the report pencil test.' (FGD Ethiopian primary school teacher)

The need to work with new technologies was considered important for keeping pace with student learning. As one Ethiopian teacher explained: "I cannot operate some equipment as well as my students ... some students, even those with poor academic achievement, learn fast when it comes to technology" (FGD, Ethiopia primary school teacher).

In India, an ongoing challenge is to pedagogically train teachers in various technologies, especially with the thrust in the National Education Policy being on blended learning and the teaching of coding in younger grades (GoI, 2020).

Teachers as innovators

Despite the lack of formal opportunities, teachers seek help from online education platforms such as DIKSHA (Government of India portal) to learn new teaching practices. Many of the respondents said that they discuss issues and concerns with peers and colleagues or people they know who are working in education, such as PhD scholars or those working with educational NGOs. Respondents said that they would like to read more research reports on pedagogic practices if given a chance. Since the teachers were not in direct contact with children during the pandemic, they tried to make videos for children and parents explaining how to do the worksheets. One of the respondents said that she seeks ideas from the curriculum and pedagogic practices of other countries such as Singapore. She specifically looks for pedagogy research reports. Others said that they revisit the notes they took during teacher training, read publications like the position reports of the National Curriculum Framework 2005 and research of the National Council for Educational Research and Training (NCERT). Some are part of social media groups of teachers where they can engage with each other. One of the respondents shared that she took a short course on pedagogy from an elite alternative private school in Delhi to enhance her pedagogic understanding and skills. In Tanzania, teachers had devised ways to stay in contact with students via their parents during the period schools were closed. The teacher educator interviewed had several ideas for improving the programme at her college and indicated some of the ways ICTs are used creatively as pedagogical tools almost as soon as they become available in a college or school.

SIX

Teacher Professionalism and the Coloniality of Being

The third dimension of Ndlovu-Gatsheni's framework, the *coloniality of being*, refers to the ways in which colonial relations are embodied at the level of personal experience in 'habits of mind and ways of being' (Adams et al, 2017), which take place in the context of, and result from, the asymmetrical power relations and knowledge systems discussed earlier (Maldonado-Torres, 2007). A focus on teachers' 'being' requires attention to the material conditions of their lives, as well as their perceptions and emotional states.

With respect to teacher professionalism, everyday realities that shape the lived experiences of the teachers in our study include: their disesteemed professional status, inadequate salary and the growing precarity of their work; the requirement to manage the unmanageable (in terms of dealing with policy contradictions, structural inequalities and conflict); their lack of agency and professional discretion in educational decision making within and beyond their immediate classroom contexts; and an emotional commitment to their work which results from its perceived importance for students and wider society.

An inadequate, undignified salary

In the colonial era, employment in medicine, engineering and law was highly restricted for indigenous people, and teaching was one of the few opportunities for relatively well-paid and secure employment within the lower rungs of the civil service hierarchy (Altbach and Kelly, 1978). Today, as our respondents explained, teaching remains a job with relatively low entrance requirements, but one for which the salary is, for the most part (India excepted), inadequate to meet the costs of living now and in the future.

Financial concerns were most serious in African contexts, where teachers' salaries are often inadequate for their needs and an ever-present source of stress. In Ethiopia, joining the teaching profession has been described as 'economic suicide' (Gemeda and Tynjälä, 2015, p 176). Teachers in our study explained that the job can provide graduates with "early employment" as a stopgap while looking for better-paid work, but that the long-term economic prospects for teachers are so poor that "experienced teachers advised their [newcomers joining their school] to take early actions to leave the profession" (FGD, Ethiopian secondary school teacher). One participant explained: "I am struggling to cover the cost for house rent and other expenses such as food and tuition fees for my kids." In Rwanda, FGD participants were less vocal on this issue, although teacher salaries in this context have long been described as a poverty wage (Rwanda, 2014), and even with the recent salary increase, government-employed primary teachers are still barely above the poverty line (Cameron, 2020). The situation is similar in Tanzania, where the majority of teachers in our study engaged in activities generating a second income in order to meet their living costs (see also Tao, 2014). This not only affects the material conditions of teachers' lives in terms of their ability to provide for themselves and dependants, but can evoke a sense of shame – that they could be better providers if they found alternative work. For example, an Ethiopian participant recounted: "I will never forget the difficult question that my kid asked me ... 'Dad! Why don't we have a good house and a car like ***' [a neighbouring engineer who works at the municipality]" (FGD, Ethiopian primary school teacher).

Although less acute outside the African continent, similar concerns around salaries were raised in the other contexts. In Colombia, participants reported that salaries "did not dignify the work of teachers". Health insurance is not guaranteed and many teachers are on temporary contracts, which means that their years of service are not fully recognized, leaving them ineligible for a pension at retirement age. Indian teachers in government schools reported that their salaries were often late, and this delay reached four to five months during the pandemic, while teachers on short-term contracts had been laid off.

In terms of the lived experience of teachers, the conditions described evoke a range of negative emotions. Many reported an acute sense of injustice that they earned less than other government employees with comparable levels of education, fewer responsibilities and additional incentives such as subsidized transport and meals. As such, many felt exploited or persecuted, while undertaking an important but impossible task (discussed later).

The sharp end of societal and systemic problems: dealing with the fallout

Of everyone in society, teachers are the group most familiar with the tensions, contradictions and inequities inherent in the mass schooling systems: irrelevant and overly challenging curricula delivered in languages many learners cannot understand; and underfunded, poorly resourced and overcrowded classrooms. Teachers in our countries of research focus operate at the sharp end of these challenges, giving them privileged knowledge and perspectives of the everyday barriers to a quality education for all. However, they also stand on the lowest rung of top-down civil service hierarchies, meaning that they recognize the challenges and contradictions of policy, but lack the decision-making authority to remedy this.

Across the board, teachers gave examples of how central policy decisions had complicated and intensified their work in unanticipated ways. For example, a Rwanda teacher explained:

'There are times when we teachers teach more than 50 hours a week. The recent policy changes from Kinyarwanda to English without corresponding teaching and learning resources has created severe teaching conditions. Some teachers have had to translate the learning content from Kinyarwanda to English before they start teaching. It is a laborious process and we lose an incredible amount of time.'

As this quote demonstrates, responding to policy changes has physical and emotional costs for teachers which are often not fully anticipated or compensated for when those higher up make seemingly technical decisions.

Among more familiar concerns raised by teachers in our study are new ones relating to the pandemic. Across the board, teachers reported growing inequalities as a result of school closures and inequitable access to out-of-school learning opportunities. In Rwanda, India, Colombia and elsewhere teachers were required to support out-of-school learning, including at weekends; however, such provision was widely considered inadequate, and teachers were fearful of what awaited them when schools reopened.

In addition, teachers have to deal with the fallout from violent conflict. The ongoing civil war in Tigray, Ethiopia, meant that the rural teachers who participated in our study were IDPs who had been given temporary accommodation in classrooms in the city. One such respondent suggested a member of our research team:

'Imagine the rural [war-stricken] areas and think where the children are these days. Many were killed, and those who escape from the perpetrators are moving from mountain to mountain, and from gorges to gorges; and are living in caves rather than their houses. Teachers are not the exception. Everything that happens to the people is also happening to teachers: torture, rape, mass killing and forced detention.' (Urban FGD, secondary school teacher, 13 June 2021)

When schools reopen it will be the responsibility of teachers to support the generation of young people who are experiencing psychosocial trauma. Similar sentiments were expressed by teachers in Colombia, where participants predicted an increase in violence in coming years despite a formal end to armed conflict (with only one, armed, actor). It is dangerous for teachers and students to move through areas where illegal armed groups are present. In some regions, the security situation aggravates the precariousness of school attendance, and forced recruitment of students by armed actors is common. Armed groups took advantage of economic needs and the lack of connectivity in the midst of the pandemic to recruit minors. In areas where the armed conflict continues, teachers may have the children of armed actors in their class, which can inhibit their ability to teach freely, create a sense of insecurity and threaten their mental health. Teachers in our sample expressed the challenge of addressing the topics of peace and conflict in class, and one (a female leader in Córdoba) had been threatened for defending children's rights.

Emotional rewards

Despite the bleak picture recounted so far, some teachers also reported positive emotions resulting from their work. This was often expressed in relation to its perceived importance. A Tanzanian teacher explained: "I am happy working as a teacher despite the many challenges I face. I usually go to the class teaching my students with enthusiasm. I don't show them that I have challenges. It is my responsibility to make sure students are well taught" (FGD, Tanzanian secondary school teacher).

Teachers also reported feeling satisfaction vicariously through the success of their students, such as this Ethiopian teacher: "I get excited when I see my former students who reached higher levels, such as becoming medical doctors, engineers and the like. I feel as if I get a return for my engagement" (FGD, Ethiopian secondary school teacher). That said, overall, viewing teacher professionalism through the lens of the *coloniality of being* reveals a systematic disregard for the material and emotional well-being of teachers. Postcolonial state structures treat teachers as dispensable or interchangeable, and their present and future living conditions as of little consequence. Within a hierarchical civil service system, teachers occupy a subservient position as foot soldiers to be directed rather than professionals whose knowledge, perspectives and judgement are of instrumental value for quality improvements in systems of mass education.

SEVEN

Towards a Practitioner-Led Understanding of Teacher Professionalism

In this concluding chapter we bring together our analysis of teachers' perspectives discussed in the previous chapters to present an overall conception of teacher professionalism. The discussion explicitly draws on the data developed through two international workshops held in June 2021 in which the participating teachers were asked to comment on the emerging findings and to identify key characteristics of teachers' professionalism in relation to these. The second aim is to relate the emerging understanding of teacher professionalism with the dominant models in the international literature and in particular the models proposed by the World Bank and by UNESCO/IE presented in the introductory section. We present our findings in relation to the latter model (which most closely encapsulates some of the views of the teachers), although we are also critical of this model.

Situating teacher professionalism

It is a central argument of the book that any understanding of teacher professionalism must be situated in an understanding of the context of teachers' work and lived experiences. This more nuanced and contextualized understanding stands in stark contrast to the one-size-fits-all approach of existing models such as the global model proposed by the World

Bank. Rather, as will be suggested, the findings are more in line with the approach of the UNESCO/IE model which argued that understanding of teaching standards and teacher professionalism must be adapted to suit different contexts. A second key argument that becomes apparent in the discussion of the situatedness of teacher professionalism is the extent to which the coloniality of power, of knowledge and of being place constraints on the possibilities for teacher professionalism compared to teachers in high-income contexts.

Figure 7.1 provides a heuristic model based on the perspectives of the teachers that captures the importance of context. Specifically, it relates the idea of teacher professionalism to the differing policy environments in each country. This includes key areas of teacher governance such as teacher pay and conditions of service but also the role of teacher unions and the lack of teacher voice in policy-making processes. It also relates, however, to the wider policy environment. Important to the discussion in previous sections are policies relating to the curriculum, pedagogy, digitization, assessment and responses to COVID-19. In the earlier discussions, the broad characteristics of the policy environment were related back to the analysis of coloniality. This includes the top-down, bureaucratic and highly centralized nature of policy but also the impact of sometimes contradictory global agendas linked to rights-based discourses (which emphasize inclusivity and sustainable development) and more economistic discourses (which emphasize privatization and the instrumental role of education in developing human capital). It was argued that teachers' own coloniality of being emerges from these wider dynamics and the contradictions inherent within them and puts constraints on their professional status, their voice in policy making and their ability to act autonomously in the classroom. The words of the teachers in this study give insights into the enduring impacts and effects of historical colonialism and also point to the 'complexly mutating entity' (Mbembe, 2016, p 32) of such legacies.

TOWARDS A PRACTITIONER-LED UNDERSTANDING

Figure 7.1: Situating teacher professionalism

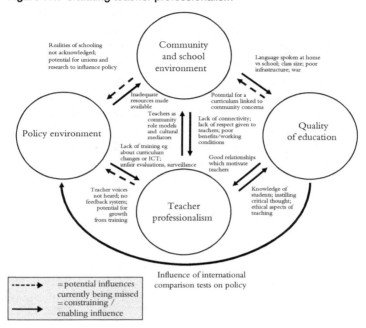

Teacher professionalism is situated in complex and nested school and community contexts which are affected by poverty and different kinds of inequality but also the impact of conflict. Importantly, the analysis draws attention to the cultural divide between home and school in linguistic and cultural terms and the role of teachers as cultural mediators. In the discussion of previous chapters, these dynamics were again linked to coloniality, including the coloniality of power, which perpetuates poverty and inequality, but also the coloniality of knowledge, which leads to a bifurcation between the modernist conception of the school and the community. The reality of teaching content that is often dislocated from local contexts and in languages that are not widely spoken in the community puts constraints on teacher autonomy in a way that is often not experienced by teachers in high-income settings but also draws attention to the tremendous skills of many teachers as cultural mediators and their importance as role models. When engaging students in any learning at all means deviating from official policies, teachers can themselves become complicit in concealing their reflexive, adaptable pedagogical expertise.

In Figure 7.1, teacher professionalism is related to differing conceptions of education quality. In discourses of the World Bank, education quality is often defined in relation to a narrow set of cognitive outcomes measured by the performance of learners in standardized assessments. By way of contrast, the teachers offered a much more holistic view of the quality of education, for example in relation to the overall well-being of learners and the rights of learners to lead sustainable livelihoods within peaceful societies. Such an understanding is more in line with the capability approach proposed by Sen (1999) and Nussbaum (2011) in which the fundamental role of education is to provide the capabilities (opportunity freedoms) required by learners to lead the lives they and their communities have reason to value. In seeking to address the capabilities of learners in their charge, teachers drew attention to the importance of their relationships with learners and communities, and their own capabilities, including their quest to develop their own professional knowledge, agency and voice. Having offered our synthesis of how teachers view their professionalism in relation to policy, community and the quality of education, in the next section we bring together their views on what teacher professionalism means in their different contexts.

Dimensions of teacher professionalism

The three dimensions of teacher professionalism proposed by UNESCO/IE provide a useful starting point for considering teachers' perspectives. A key argument developed in this section is that the teachers' perspectives provide a grounded, contextualized understanding of each dimension that can complement global understandings such as those proposed by UNESCO and Education International.

Teaching knowledge and understanding

It will be recalled that the UNESCO/IE framework emphasizes the importance of teacher expertise in subject knowledge and their abilities to teach specific subjects (often referred to in the literature as pedagogical content knowledge). The teachers involved in this study endorsed the importance of subject and pedagogical content knowledge. For example, they emphasized, in keeping with global agendas, their own need to upgrade their skills and knowledge in specific subject areas such as STEM and, particularly in the context of the COVID-19 pandemic, the use of digital technologies. The teachers across the five contexts also highlighted the importance of knowledge and skills linked to sustainable futures. These included an emphasis on relevant vocational skills, environmental understanding, peace and citizenship education, and the value of arts and culture education for developing learners as fully rounded human beings. Missing from the UNESCO/IE model is the crucial importance of teachers not only as receivers and transmitters of knowledge but also as potential creators of knowledge. In particular, the teachers emphasized their role in developing a better understanding of the realities of teaching and learning in the challenging contexts in which they often operated.

Teaching practice

It will be recalled that this domain concerns educators' ability to engage with their learners. In global discourses, this is often related to ideas about teacher effectiveness and the ability of teachers to improve learning outcomes in high-stakes examinations and international comparison tests. As mentioned, however, the teachers largely rejected this understanding of their effectiveness and instead offered a more holistic interpretation of the outcomes of education and the meaning of education quality. A key consideration was the ability to relate and adapt curricula to the backgrounds and needs of the learners, and this, in turn, required detailed knowledge and understanding of local contexts and realities. Even the way teachers introduced and talked about the limitations of the curriculum and the challenges of classroom teaching demonstrated reflexive practitioner knowledge. They did not speak about their pupils and students as anonymous 'learners' but as children and young people. They knew about the homes they lived in, where they were when schools were closed, and were aware of young people's aspirations for their futures.

There were differences between countries in the breadth of teachers' vocabulary for talking about pedagogy, with teachers in India and Columbia demonstrating greater pedagogical content knowledge than participants from the three African countries. However, this disparity may indicate the distance between the realities of classroom conditions in the three African countries and the Western discourses of professionalism that slide between personalized and performative pedagogy. A key aspect of teaching practice that is often not relayed in the global literature is the crucial role of teachers as cultural mediators and community leaders. This not only entails seeking to bridge the gap between the standardized knowledge contained in centralized curricula but also in being able to mediate between the home languages spoken by the learners and the medium of teaching and learning, which is often a global language. In the context of increasingly heterogeneous learning environments, this requires the ability to respond positively to cultural diversity. It also requires exceptional linguistic capital on the part of teachers. In the research, teachers mediated in the opposite direction, articulating for researchers the aspirations, opportunities and constraints experienced by students. Finally, the teachers often emphasized their important role in safeguarding the welfare of their students, including through their skills as counsellors and career advisors.

Teaching relations

The third dimension of the UNESCO/IE model focuses on the central importance of relationships with students, fellow professionals, caregivers and educational authorities. In relation to parents and communities, the teachers emphasized their role as socializing agents, involving their ability to inculcate acceptable societal values, citizenship and a love for lifelong learning. They talked about the importance of having high expectations for all learners. They emphasized their position as role models and the importance of values such as honesty, fairness and humility. The teachers also highlighted the importance of collegial relationships that were often challenged by the emphasis under neoliberalism on performativity, competition and surveillance. Finally, and in contrast to the top-down view of professionalism that is often evident in global agendas and realities, the teachers unanimously emphasized the importance of their voice in policy making. This was considered important as a means for advocating teachers' rights to decent pay and conditions of service and to have their professional status recognized. Crucially, however, the teachers stressed the importance of their perspectives for effective policy implementation and as a means to improve the quality of education for their learners.

Conclusion

The book has sought to make a contribution to the decolonization of teacher professionalism. This is done through using a decolonial lens to critique dominant global discourses concerning teacher professionalism and by foregrounding the perspectives of teachers in the global South against a situated understanding of the diverse and often extremely challenging contexts in which they work. Through the course of the book, we have sought to develop several key arguments. These include the importance of situating any understanding of teacher professionalism against an understanding of the diverse contexts in which teachers around the world currently operate and to use this understanding to push back against the tendency to promote one-size-fits-all models of teacher professionalism. We have sought to argue the value of a decolonial approach towards understanding how the coloniality of power and of knowledge impact on the coloniality of being of teachers, constraining their professional standing and autonomy. Nonetheless, and in contrast to some dominant global agendas, we have explicitly rejected a deficit view of teacher professionalism in the global South. While recognizing the barriers and constraints to teacher professionalism, we have also sought to highlight the tremendous resourcefulness and resilience of teachers, the full range of their capacities, skills and dispositions as well as their commitment to their profession and to the well-being of their learners. Here there is much that global discourses can learn from the lived experiences of teachers in the global South.

We recognize, however, the exploratory nature of our study and the constraints imposed on the research by the demanding time frames involved and the difficulties of conducting research in the context of a pandemic. The study is based on work with a small sample of teachers in each of the countries of focus. Thus, while we are confident that our study provides useful, contextualized understanding that can add value to existing debates, it is not intended to be definitive or fully representative of teachers' views in these countries. Further quantitative and qualitative research might usefully develop some of the insights generated to involve a greater number of teachers and in more diverse contexts. In conducting our research, we have sought to illustrate the potential for actively engaging teachers in the research process as co-creators of knowledge about their own professionalism. It is suggested that engaging teachers in this

TOWARDS A PRACTITIONER-LED UNDERSTANDING

way not only provides an antidote to the often extractive and top-down approach that characterizes much of the research into teacher professionalism but also serves to positively illustrate the importance of engaging teachers' perspectives for taking forward global debates.

EIGHT

Conflict in Tigray: Teachers' Experiences and the Implications for Post-Conflict Reconstruction

Nigusse Weldemariam Reda and Rafael Mitchell

The Ethiopian strand of our cross-national research took place in Tigray during a devastating civil conflict. This supplementary chapter draws on testimonies and artefacts shared by teachers as part of fieldwork in 2021, and reports on their experiences of trauma, displacement, the destruction of lives and schools, and the implications for the teaching profession in the years ahead.

In November 2020 conflict erupted between the forces of the federal government of Ethiopia and those of Tigray's ruling party, the Tigrayan People's Liberation Front. Over more than two years, hundreds of thousands of civilians have been killed, and many millions displaced and subjected to a weaponized famine (Mulugeta and Gebregziabher, 2022; UN, 2022). The region has been besieged and cut off from the outside world for extended periods, with electricity, telephones, banking and other public services suspended. Following a Cessation of Hostilities Agreement in November 2022, the situation is beginning to stabilize, and at the time of writing (early 2023), we are at the start of a long road to recovery.

The school system in Tigray, which developed over the past three decades to achieve near-universal primary enrolment, has been devastated by the war (HRW and AI, 2021). In terms of educational infrastructure, the latest available data suggest that almost 90 per cent of classrooms have been damaged (Tigray Education Bureau, 2021), while the human cost of the conflict to school communities is beyond reckoning. The widespread atrocities against civilians and telecoms blackouts have posed a challenge to the production of systematic evidence on the state of the school system in the region. For example, the high-profile Research on Improving Systems of Education (RISE) Ethiopia research programme dropped Tigray from its sample due to security concerns (Bayley et al, 2021). This gives particular value to the evidence collected from teachers as part of the *Decolonising Teacher Professionalism* study, given the key role that teachers will need to play in efforts to rebuild schooling in the region over the coming years. This chapter presents a thematic analysis of the testimonies and artefacts shared by ten teachers during fieldwork in Mekelle in April 2021. Of these, five were teachers from rural schools who had been internally displaced by the conflict. This chapter expands on the previous analysis to explore the distinct challenges which the profession faces as a result of the conflict. In the first sections of this chapter we report on teachers' experiences of trauma and displacement and the destruction of lives and schools. We close by considering the implications of the conflict for the teaching profession in the years ahead.

Teachers as civilians: trauma and displacement

Everyone in Tigray has suffered as a result of the conflict. The teachers interviewed for this study faced the same privations as other civilians in the region. As one teacher explained: "everything that happens to the people is also happening to teachers: displacement, torture, rape, mass killing and forced detention" (Urban teacher, male, 13 June 2021). Teachers shared experiences of *psychological trauma* and the effects of *displacement*.

The abrupt outbreak of war, its speed and the behaviour of the warring parties induced psychological shock in the people of Tigray. Although the political environment had been increasingly turbulent since 2018, civilians were not psychologically prepared for war. One teacher explained: "I never thought a war could happen and I was shocked when I heard the news. ... Especially, for people who live from hand-to-mouth, the eruption of the war immersed us into a dead shock" (Urban teacher, primary school teacher, 13 June 2021).

At the start of hostilities, the regional government declared a curfew, prohibiting the movement of civilians within the region and beyond, while the federal government advised Tigrayans not to gather close to war zones, military camps or fuel stations. An elementary schoolteacher remembered: "Every human activity was stumbled by fear ... Even going to the market to get groceries was difficult ... An air raid could happen at any point in time" (Rural teacher, male, 19 June 2021).

Within a few days, the military engagement become full-fledged and multi-frontal, encompassing air and drone strikes, and exchange of short- and medium-range arms fire (Teka, 2021). The heavy bombardments led to long-standing psychological scars among the civilian population. One teacher shared how this affected his family: "My daughter rushes to hide herself under any cover whenever she hears loud sounds, such as the sound of a car, door, and airplane" (Rural teacher, male, 19 June 2021).

The acts of invading forces have been described as ethnic cleansing and crimes against humanity (HRW and AI, 2022; UN, 2022), including mass killings and the forced displacement, detention and torture of civilians. News of atrocities spread fear across the population, with many in rural areas leaving home to seek sanctuary in urban centres. Mekelle, the regional capital, became a temporary home for thousands of IDPs, who were housed in schools and other makeshift shelters, including the classrooms where our fieldwork took place. Rural schoolteachers shared horrifying experiences of trauma from their journeys.

> 'On our way from Western Tigray to Mekelle, we saw many inhuman things which I will never forget. Dead bodies scattered on the ground! Injured people that sought immediate care and attention … Some were hit by shrapnel from bombardments, while others [had been] slaughtered by the perpetrators.' (Rural teacher, male, 19 June 2021)

On reaching IDP centres, hardships continued due to a lack of food, medication and other materials. Like other state employees, teachers did not receive their salaries over this period and faced destitution. One teacher shared experiences of "sleeping on the floor without a blanket. Spending your day without a meal is common in almost all IDP centres" (Rural teacher, female, 19 June 2021). Another explained: "I am living in a tent that has nothing to eat and drink. I saw how the future of the people-like mine got lost in daylight" (Rural teacher, female, 19 June 2021).

Teachers as horrified spectators: the devastation of school infrastructure

The teachers described the widespread destruction of school infrastructure in Tigray as a result of direct bombardment or damage incurred through the repurposing of school buildings for military or civilian uses. One rural teacher shared a photograph of her former school which had been hit by a shell (see Figure 8.1).

> 'As I was [escaping] from my home to Mekelle, I stopped in the area where I used to live and teach. [When I saw] my school I was horrified. It had been bombed and almost every item of school property (including chairs and blackboards) was looted, broken and thrown outside.' (Rural teacher, female, 19 June 2021)

Figure 8.1: School building hit by heavy shell

Where schools had been occupied by the military there were fears that unexploded mines may have been left behind, alongside tattered and bloody uniforms, and dangerous medical or military equipment (HRW and AI, 2021). School infrastructure was also damaged through military searches and looting. For example, a secondary schoolteacher reported that federal soldiers had ransacked his school office to search for hidden materials (see Figure 8.2): "[When I reached my school] I saw a strange thing – almost everything was damaged: equipment, teaching materials, and individual properties were looted, disarranged and destroyed. What a day!" (Urban teacher, male, 13 June 2021).

Because of this, schools had lost their archives (for example, students' marks, exams, worksheets); specialist resources such as laboratories, libraries and ICT equipment; and essential classroom equipment including chairs, desks and blackboards.

Figure 8.2: School records destroyed during the conflict

The use of school buildings as IDP shelters also resulted in damage (see Figure 8.3). One displaced elementary teacher explained:

'The school where I live is full to the brim [with IDPs]. All classrooms, including the laboratory and libraries are used as living rooms. So, you cannot blame these people: they throw away or break the educational materials either to get space, or to use them for their living essentials such as cooking, sitting and sleeping.' (Rural teacher, female, 19 June 2021)

Teachers were deeply affected by the destruction of school resources; they knew the work which had gone into securing these over many years, and the consequences of their destruction.

'Teachers have a professional attachment to the school and its resources. They know the effort that a school has invested in getting its resources and, at the same time, the value of educational resources in supporting

Figure 8.3: A classroom used to house IDPs (this is the original photo of an occupied classroom, taken during the civil war)

the teaching and learning process ... Teachers then lose their hope in the profession, and they find it chilling to see school resources that they once used ... being thrown away, broken, looted, etc.' (Rural teacher, female, 19 June 2021)

Clearly, major reconstruction work is needed to make school facilities in Tigray serviceable again. What plans and resources will be available for this, and what will it mean for the teaching profession? Early indications were provided during fieldwork when the short-lived federal-backed interim government ordered the reopening of schools in June 2021. As one teacher explained, the basic conditions for teaching and learning were not in place, and the onus seemed to be on teachers to make any arrangements necessary without appropriate support.

'The interim government is announcing to reopen schools, but almost all schools have been looted or demolished. I do not know in which classrooms we are going to teach [or] what kind of teaching we [can] handle, without textbooks, laboratory equipment ... After all, the environment is not yet safe ... Let alone to go to school, I am terrified to go an inch outside of my house.' (Urban teacher, male, 13 June 2021)

If past experience is a guide, there are likely to be strong expectations around teachers' and communities' direct involvement in efforts to restore school infrastructure and resources, a point we return to later.

The effects of the conflict on young people

Teachers recounted the appalling effects of the conflict on young people in the region. At the time of writing, comprehensive data on civilian casualties of the war and associated siege and famine are unavailable, but it is certain that many thousands have died as a direct or indirect result of the conflict, and survivors are widely affected by malnutrition, a lack of medication and trauma (Gesesew et al, 2021; Mulugeta and Gebregziabher, 2022). Many families had been separated through the conflict. "[In the IDP centres] there are many children who do not have information about their family, and many families that don't have information about their children either" (Rural teacher, female, 19 June 2021). Efforts to locate or reunite missing family members were hindered by the ongoing fighting and blockade.

Teachers reported changes in young people's attitudes towards formal education since the start of the conflict, with growing scepticism about its value, and the prospects of schools reopening.

'Whenever you ask a student about how life is, and whether he or she is studying, he responds with audacity: 'Do you think the schools are reopened?' Students have convinced themselves that it will take a long time to reopen schools … They even tell you that the value of education is meaningless in such a war-torn environment.' (Rural teacher, female, 19 June 2021)

This sense of futility echoes that of young people in neighbouring Amhara region, where schooling has also been disrupted by the conflict. Based on interviews with young people in Amhara, Jones and colleagues (2022, p 6) report that 'educational aspirations had shifted as a result of the war … [and] even young people in mid-adolescence were losing interest in schooling and eager to contribute to the war effort'. A secondary teacher in our study explained that some young people felt an inevitability around joining the fighting:

'When the political tension between the federal and the regional government was popping, you saw an immediate deterioration in the attention of students. Now and then, you hear students chatting about it and … a number of students say: that, "One day [or another,] becoming a military man is unavoidable".' (Urban teacher, male, 13 June 2021)

Students and their parents were preoccupied with the developments of the war inside and outside Tigray. One discussant shared that everyone, from "children to the elderly developed [an obsession]: 'what's new today?'" (Rural teacher, female, 19 June 2021). The economic hardships resulting from the siege shifted the focus of parents and their children from questions of learning to those of survival. Teachers anticipated that this would cause long-term disruption to young people's education – as one explained: "Students can forget the contents of their curriculum even under normal occasions … let alone in the event of a war which provokes fear and trauma" (Urban teacher, male, 13 June 2021).

Implications for the profession in post-conflict reconstruction

In this final section we draw on the earlier evidence, alongside the wider literature on education in conflict, to consider the implications of the war for the teaching profession in Tigray. The discussion is organized in three broad areas: mobilizing the education workforce; reconstructing school infrastructure; and reimagining schooling in ways which respond to the trauma experienced by people in Tigray and offer a positive vision for the future.

Mobilizing the education workforce

The teaching profession in Tigray, Ethiopia, was facing serious, intractable challenges even before the present conflict with respect to teachers' economic status (Mitchell, 2017, p 111), their lack of agency and influence on issues affecting their practice (Ahmed and Mihiretie, 2015; Taddese and Rao, 2021; Weigele and Brandt, 2022), and the material conditions of teaching and learning, especially in rural areas. These conditions have only worsened due to the conflict.

The teaching workforce has been shattered by the conflict. Many teachers have been physically displaced from the communities where they worked, and across the region there has been a general movement from rural to urban areas. It is unclear how the post-conflict reconstruction will affect the distribution of people over the coming years, and the extent to which people will be able, or willing, to return to the areas where they lived previously. In addition to this, the suspension of teachers' salaries for more than a year has led many to find alternative means of employment. For schools across the region to reopen, policy actors will have to find ways to entice qualified teachers to return to the profession, *and* physically relocate to where they are needed. In the short term, this could include financial incentives, and the provision of transport, food and home supplies. But in the longer term, it will rely on policy actors providing an attractive salary and working conditions, job security and a clear path to career progression (Sayed et al, 2018).

Nevertheless, it is unlikely that educational demands can be met solely by reappointing former teachers, as post-conflict contexts elsewhere in the region have found (Novelli and Higgins, 2017; Sayed et al, 2018). The traditional route to training new teachers has been disrupted by the closure of Tigray's two teacher training institutions since the start of the conflict, and building surveys show that these sites were heavily damaged in the war (Tigray Education Bureau, 2021). It is likely that addressing staffing shortages will require the appointment of unqualified teachers, such as university or high school graduates. While this may be necessary to address immediate needs, joined-up strategies are required for the initial training and ongoing mentoring and support of such teachers, along with pathways to formal certification (Sayed et al, 2018; Bengtsson et al, 2020). Decisions in these areas will have lasting implications for the quality of education and the long-term status of the profession.

Reconstructing school infrastructure

Many schools had inadequate infrastructure prior to the conflict: shortages of desks, seats and basic teaching materials were common, with less than half of schools in the region having library facilities or access to running water (Mitchell, 2017, p 20). Government support has never been sufficient to fully fund primary provision, particularly in rural areas, and cost-sharing policies were introduced in the 2000s to make progress on policy commitments for universal primary enrolment (Oumer, 2009). As a result, many schools in Tigray were constructed by their local communities through the contribution of fees, materials and labour; and the varying capacity of locals to provide such support led to wide disparities in the nature and quality of infrastructure across the region (Agegnehu, 2017; Tiruneh et al, 2021). An appreciation of this context is necessary to understand the despair expressed by teachers over the destruction of school buildings and equipment, causing some to "lose hope in the profession", as one rural teacher put it. Communities impoverished by the conflict will have limited resources to contribute to the restoration of school infrastructure, and so reconstruction will be reliant on additional investment from the state and external agencies such as the World Bank, which has committed $300 million for conflict-affected areas nationally, including Tigray (World Bank, 2022). To avoid reproducing stark disparities in the quality of school infrastructure, it will be important for policy actors to take an equity-oriented approach to resource distribution (Novelli et al, 2019), which may involve directing additional funds towards schools in historically underserved communities and incentives for teachers serving in such areas.

Reimagining schooling

Teachers will play a key role in post-conflict reconstruction, in terms of responding to the psychological trauma which young people in Tigray have experienced (Gebre and Hagos, 2023) and contributing to wider peacebuilding efforts. For example, research in Liberia during the post-conflict era found teachers taking on multiple new roles, as 'second parents, humanitarians, "town criers", role models, guardians, parents, counsellors, unifiers, agents of peace, "Hercules", and psychologists to help students suffering from post-traumatic stress disorder' (Adebayo, 2019, p 1).

As we have seen from the earlier accounts, teachers in Tigray are likely to face similar demands. As state-employed professionals in regular contact with traumatized young people, providing counselling and other forms of psychosocial support would not be inappropriate, if it is accompanied by the necessary training, support and recognition (Mwoma and Pillay, 2015; Sayed et al, 2018). Unfortunately, such conditions are unusual, as despite the prevalence of conflict-related trauma across the continent, Musisi and Kinyanda (2020, p 9) note a 'virtual absence of post-conflict mental health policies in almost all African countries'.

In terms of the peacebuilding function of education, a restoration of the pre-conflict status quo is neither possible nor wholly desirable. The conflict in Tigray occurred *despite* record levels of participation in formal education, and the proliferation of inter-ethnic and gender-based violence indicates that the school system is not achieving its objectives in terms of developing a peaceful, inclusive society. A positive vision for schooling in the post-conflict era requires an honest and comprehensive assessment of the conditions which led to the conflict, and the changes needed for a sustained peace that is grounded in social justice for all (Novelli et al, 2019). As discussed earlier, this will necessarily involve some element of *redistribution*, to ensure a more equitable distribution of resources and opportunities. It will also require finding ways to teach about the conflict and its legacies in ways that may lead to *reconciliation* (Novelli et al, 2019). This is an agenda for the coming years.

Appendix

Table A.1: Data collection in the country contexts

Country context	Forms of data collection carried out
Colombia	**Focus group discussions** with 12 primary and secondary schoolteachers from 11 different regions of the country. Six teach in rural schools, one in semi-rural and five in urban schools. **Interviews**: (1) representative from the teacher union federation, *Federación Colombiana de Trabajadores de la Educación* (FECODE); (2) advisor from Institute for Educational Research and Pedagogical Development (Instituto para la Investigación Educativa y el Desarrollo Pedaagógico, IDEP); and (3) teacher from the Universidad Distrital, Bogotá, and advisor to the Ministry of Education. **Focus group discussion** with two secondary school students.
Ethiopia	**Focus group discussions** with ten teachers from Tigray region: five teachers from secondary schools in Mekelle; five teachers from rural and semi-rural areas (four primary, one secondary) who were internally displaced due to the conflict. **Interviews:** (i) two representatives from the Teachers Association, (ii) one representative from university-based teacher education programme.
India	**Focus group discussion** with nine teachers from state schools in Delhi. **Pedagogic artefacts**: one from each of the nine teachers. **Anecdotes of practice**: one from each of the nine teachers.

(continued)

Table A.1: Data collection in the country contexts (continued)

Country context	Forms of data collection carried out
	Additional data: all nine teachers collated data from a total of 28 additional teachers in state schools, largely through individual interviews and some via group discussions with two to three teachers.
Rwanda	**Focus group discussions** with nine teachers and one teacher training college instructor. The group included four primary school teachers and five secondary school teachers. Those teachers provided additional data collected, including pedagogic artefacts from eight of their colleagues, including four primary teachers and four secondary school teachers. **Interviews**: one official who has worked in the field of teacher professionalization and development.
Tanzania	**Focus group discussions or one-on-one interviews** (due to connectivity issues) conducted online with nine teachers, with six from primary schools and six from secondary schools. Nine taught in rural settings and three taught in urban settings. **Interviews**: (1) a teacher educator from a teacher training college; (2) a researcher from a large, influential education advocacy and policy-influencing organization.

Notes

one Introduction: The Case for Decolonizing Teacher Professionalism

[1] The book is based on a background paper prepared for the UNESCO Futures of the Teaching Profession Initiative (Tikly et al, 2023). The authors wish to acknowledge their gratitude to UNESCO for granting permission for the material contained in the paper to be reproduced in this book.

[2] The term 'global South' is used as shorthand terminology to signify formerly colonized, low- and middle-income countries, including those of research focus. Caution is needed, however, in the use of this terminology so as not to homogenize the histories and current realities facing these countries. As we discuss later, for example, the countries of research focus have very different experiences of colonialism and represent very different economic, political, social, demographic, cultural and educational realities.

four Teacher Professionalism and the Coloniality of Power

[1] Although not explicitly discussed in this book, it is also essential to recognize pre-colonial histories of education in each of the countries of research focus.

[2] This is increasingly contested by the so-called rising powers, namely Brazil, Russia, India, China and South Africa.

[3] In this regard, the Westphalian model needs to be understood as an idealized model, as issues of corruption and nepotism are also evident in high-income Western societies that are supposedly based on the model.

References

Acevedo Terazona, A. (2013) 'Traces, resonances and lessons of the pedagogical movement in Colombia', *Praxis and Saber*, 4(8): 63–85.

Adams, G., Estrada-Villalta, S. and Gómez Ordóñez, L. (2017) 'The modernity/coloniality of being: hegemonic psychology as intercultural relations', *International Journal of Intercultural Relations*, https://doi.org/10.1016/j.ijintrel.2017.06.006.

Adebayo, S.B. (2019) 'Emerging perspectives of teacher agency in a post-conflict setting: the case of Liberia', *Teaching and Teacher Education*, https://doi.org/10.1016/j.tate.2019.102928.

Agegnehu, A. (2017) 'The practice of decentralized education service delivery: an impact assessment – the case of Ganta-Afeshum Woreda – eastern zone of Tigray state', *Ethiopian Journal of Social Sciences and Language Studies*, 4(2): 81–109.

Ahmed, A.Y. and Mihiretie, D.M. (2015) 'Primary school teachers and parents' views on automatic promotion practices and its implications for education quality', *International Journal of Educational Development*, 43: 90–99.

Aikman, S. (2011) 'Educational and indigenous justice in Africa', *International Journal of Educational Development*, 31(1): 15–22.

Altbach, P. and Kelly, G. (1978) *Education and Colonialism*, New York: Longman.

Amin, S. (1997) *Capitalism in the Age of Globalisation*, London: Zed Books.

Annys, S. et al (2021) *Tigray: Atlas of the Humanitarian Situation*, Ghent: Ghent University.

Ashley, L.D. et al (2014) *The Role and Impact of Private Schools in Developing Countries*, London: DfID.

Avalos, B.B. (2013) 'Teacher professionalism and social justice', in L.B. Tikly (ed) *Education Quality and Social Justice in the South: Challenges for Policy, Practice and Research*, London: Routledge, pp 35–52.

Bahru, Z. (2002) *Pioneers of Change in Ethiopia*, Athens: Ohio University Press.

REFERENCES

Ball, S.J. (2003) 'The teacher's soul and the terrors of performativity', *Journal of Education Policy*, 18(2): 215–228, https://doi.org/10.1080/0268093022000043065

Ball, S.J. (2008) 'New philanthropy, new networks and new governance in education', *Political Studies*, 56(4): 747–765.

Ball, S.J. (2015) 'Education, governance and the tyranny of numbers', *Journal of Education Policy*, 30(3): 299–301.

Ball, S.J. and Youdell, D. (2008) *Hidden Privatisation in Public Education*, Geneva: Education International.

Barrett, A.M. (2008) 'Capturing the différance: primary school teacher identity in Tanzania', *International Journal of Educational Development*, 28(5): 496–507.

Batra, P. (2014) 'Problematising teacher education practice in India: developing a research agenda', *Education as Change*, 18(sup1): S5–S18.

Batra, P. (2020) 'Echoes of "coloniality" in the episteme of Indian educational reforms', *On Education. Journal for Research and Debate*, 3(7): 1–17.

Bayley, S., Wole, D., Ramchandani, P., Rose, P., Woldehanna, T. and Yorke, L. (2021) 'Socio-Emotional and Academic Learning before and after COVID-19 School Closures: Evidence from Ethiopia', RISE Working Paper Series, 21/082, https://doi.org/10.35489/BSG-RISE-WP_2021/082.

Bengtsson, S., Fitzpatrick, R., Hinz, K., MacEwen, L., Naylor, R., Riggall, A. et al (2020) *Teacher Management in Refugee Settings*, Ethiopia. Education Development Trust.

Benson, C. (2014) 'Designing effective schooling in multi-lingual contexts: going beyond bilingual models', in T. Skutnabb-Kangas et al (eds) *Social Justice Through Multilingual Education*, Toronto: Multilingual Matters, pp 63–84.

Béteille, T. and Evans, D. (2021) *Successful Teachers, Successful Students: Recruiting and Supporting Society's Most Crucial Profession*, Washington: World Bank.

Boas, M. and McNeill, D. (2004) *Global Institutions and Development – Framing the World?*, London: Routledge.

Bravo, A.M. (2015) 'Fragmentos de la Historia del Conflicto Armado (1920–2010)', Bogota: Espacio Critico.

Buchert, L. (1994) *Education in the Development of Tanzania*, Athens: Ohio University Press.

Buchert, L. (2002) 'Education for all: an attainable dream?', *Prospects*, XXXII(1): 25–48.

Bullough, R.V. (2001) 'Pedagogical content knowledge circa 1907 and 1987: a study in the history of an idea', *Teaching and Teacher Education*, 17(6): 655–666.

Cameron, L.M. (2020) *'Looking Out': Neoliberal Discourses and English Language Teacher Professionalism in Rwanda*, University of Bristol, Bristol, London: Inter-agency Network for Education in Emergencies (INEE) & the Alliance for Child Protection in Humanitarian Action (ACPHA).

Cameron, L.M. (2021) 'No Education, No Protection: What School Closures under COVID-19 Mean for Children and Young People in Crisis-Affected Contexts', London: Inter-agency Network for Education in Emergencies (INEE) & the Alliance for Child Protection in Humanitarian Action (ACPHA).

Castellanos, M.B. (2017) 'Introduction: settler colonialism in Latin America', *American Quarterly*, 69(4): 777–781.

Castells, M. (2000) *Information Technology and Global Development*, Paris: Economic and Social Council of the United Nations.

Clegg, J. and Afitska, O. (2011) 'Teaching and learning in two languages in African classrooms', *Comparative Education*, 47(1): 61–77.

Clegg, J. and Simpson, J. (2016) 'Improving the effectiveness of English as a medium of instruction in sub-Saharan Africa', *Comparative Education*, 52(3): 359–374.

Comoroff, J. and Comoroff, J. (2011) *Theory from the South: Or, How Euro-America Is Evolving towards Africa*, Boulder, CO: Paradigm.

Connelly, F.M. and Clandinin, D.J. (1990) 'Stories of experience and narrative inquiry', *Educational Researcher*, 19(5): 2–14.

Cortez Ochoa, A.A., Tikly, L., Hutchinson, Y., Paulson, J., and Sriprakash, A. (2021) Synthesis Report on the Decolonising Education for Sustainable Futures (UNESCO Chair seminar series), Bristol Conversations in Education & UNESCO Chair Seminar Series.

REFERENCES

Crawfurd, L. and Hares, S. (2020) 'There's a global school sexual violence crisis and we don't know enough about it', Blog post, [online] 6 March. Available from: www.cgdev.org/blog/theres-global-school-sexual-violence-crisis-and-we-dont-know-eno ugh-about-it [Accessed 6 January 2024].

Crossley, M. (2019) 'Policy transfer, sustainable development and the contexts of education', *Compare: A Journal of Comparative and International Education*, 49(2): 175–191.

Crossley, M., Vaka'uta, C., Lagi, R., McGrath, S., Thaman, K., and Waqailiti, L. (2017) 'Quality education and the role of the teacher in Fiji: mobilising global and local values', *Compare: A Journal of Comparative and International Education*, 47(6): 872–890.

Dale, R. (1989) *The State and Education Policy*, Milton Keynes: Open University Press.

Darder, A. (2017) *Reinventing Paulo Freire: A Pedagogy of Love*, London: Taylor and Francis.

Dixon, K. (2019) *Searching for Mermaids: Access, Capital, and the Digital Divide in a Rural South African Primary School*, London: Routledge.

Dunne, M. and Leach, F. (2005) *Gendered School Experiences: The Impact of Retention and Achievement in Botswana and Ghana*, London: DfID.

Erling, E., Clegg, J., Rubagumya, C., and Reilly, C. (eds) (2021) *Multilingual Learning and Language Supportive Pedagogies in Sub-Saharan Africa*, London: Routledge.

Escobar, A. (2004) 'Development, violence and the new imperial order', *Development*, 47(1): 15–21.

Escobar, A. (2014) *Encountering Development*, Princeton NJ: Princeton University Press.

Etzoini, A. (1969) *The Semi-Professions: Teachers, Nurses, Social Workers*, New York: Free Press.

Evans, L. (2008) 'Professionalism, professionality and the development of education professionals', *British Journal of Educational Studies*, 56(1): 20–38.

FAO (Food and Agricultural Organisation) (2020) 'The State of Food Security and Nutrition in the World 2020: Transforming Food Systems for Affordable Healthy Diets', Rome: FAO.

Ferguson, J. (2006) *Global Shadows: Africa in the Neoliberal World Order*, Durham, NC: Duke University Press.

Frank, A. (1970) *Latin America: Underdevelopment or Revolution*, New York: Monthly Review Press.

Friere, P. (1970) *Pedagogy of the Oppressed*, London: Penguin.

Furlong, J., Barton, L., Miles, S., Whiting, C. and Whitty, G. (2000) *Teacher Education in Transition*, Milton Keynes: Open University Press.

Gebre, A.H. and Hagos, B. (2023) 'Education is a humanitarian imperative for children in Tigray, Ethiopia', GPE (Global Partnership for Education), [online]. Available from: www.global partnership.org/blog/education-humanitarian-imperative-child ren-tigray-ethiopia [Accessed 27 November 2023].

Gemeda, F. and Tynjälä, P. (2015) 'Exploring teachers' motivation for teaching and professional development in Ethiopia: voices from the field', *Journal of Studies in Education*, 5: 169.

Gesesew, H., Berhane, K., Siraj, E.S., Siraj, D., Gebregziabher, M., Gebre, Y.G. et al (2021) 'The impact of war on the health system of the Tigray region in Ethiopia: an assessment', *BMJ Global Health*, 6: e007328.

GoI (1986) National Policy on Education, Delhi: Government of India.

GoI (2020) National Education Policy 2020, Delhi: Government of India.

Goodwin, A.L. (2020) 'Teaching standards, globalisation, and conceptions of teacher professionalism', *European Journal of Teacher Education*, 44(1): 5–19.

Govender, L., Hoffman, N. and Sayed, Y. (2016) 'Teacher Professionalism and Accountability', Cape Town: Centre for International Teacher Education.

Grace, G. (1987) 'Teachers and the state in Britain: a changing relation', in M. Lawn and G. Grace (eds) *Teachers: The Culture and Politics of Work*, Brighton: Falmer Press, pp 193–228.

Gray, K. and Murphy, C.N. (2013) 'Introduction: rising powers and the future of global governance', *Third World Quarterly*, 34(2): 183–193.

Hargreaves, A. (2000) 'Four ages of professionalism and professional learning', *Teachers and Teaching*, 6(2): 151–182.

REFERENCES

Harvey, D. (2003) *The New Imperialism*, Oxford: Oxford University Press.

Herbst, J. (2000) *States and Power in Africa: Comparative Lessons in Authority and Control*, Princeton, NJ: Princeton University Press.

Hoogvelt, A. (1997) *Globalisation and the Postcolonial World*, London: Macmillan Press.

Horner, L. et al (2015) 'Literature Review: The Role of Teachers in Peacebuilding', Bristol: University of Bristol.

HRW (2021) 'Ethiopia: Tigray Schools Occupied, Looted', Human Rights Watch, [online] 28 May. Available from: www.hrw.org/news/2021/05/28/ethiopia-tigray-schools-occupied-looted [Accessed 17 January 2023].

HRW and AI (2022) ' "We Will Erase You from This Land": Crimes against Humanity and Ethnic Cleansing in Ethiopia's Western Tigray Zone', Human Rights Watch and Amnesty International, [online] June. Retrieved from: www.hrw.org/sites/default/files/media_2 022/06/ethiopia0422_web_0.pdf [Accessed 17 January 2023].

Hutchinson, Y., Ochoa, A., Paulson, J. and Tikly, L. (eds) (2023) *Decolonizing Education for Sustainable Futures*, Bristol: Bristol University Press.

ILO (International Labour Organisation) (1996) 'Impact of Structural Adjustment on the Employment and Training of Teachers: Report for Discussion at the Joint Meeting on the Impact of Structural Adjustment on Educational Personnel', Geneva: ILO.

ILO/UNESCO (1966) 'Recommendation Concerning the Status of Teachers', Geneva: ILO.

Jean, V. (2020) 'International aid to education: power dynamics in an era of partnership', *International Review of Education*, 66(2–3): 431–433.

Johnson, S., Monk, M. and Hodges, M. (2000) 'Teacher development and change in South Africa: a critique of the appropriateness of transfer of northern/western practice', *Compare*, 30(2): 179–192.

Jones, N., Abebe, W., Emirie, G., Gebeyehu, Y., Gezahegne, K., Kassahun Tilahun, K., et al (2022) 'Disrupted educational pathways: the effects of conflict on adolescent educational access and learning in war-torn Ethiopia', *Frontiers in Education*, 7: 963415.

Kahler, M. (2013) 'Rising powers and global governance: negotiating change in a resilient status quo', *International Affairs (Royal Institute of International Affairs 1944–)*, 89(3): 711–729, www.jstor.org/stable/23473851

Kasuga, W. (2019) Teaching profession in Tanzania: unequal profession among the equal professions, *International Journal of Recent Innovations in Academic Research*, 3(4): 86–106.

King-Hill, S. (2021) 'How to … tackle "rape culture" in schools', *Times Educational Supplement*, 25 June.

Komba, S.C. and Mwakabenga, R.J. (2020) 'Teacher professional development in Tanzania: challenges and opportunities', in *Educational Leadership*, IntechOpen, pp 1–12.

Lavia, J. (2006) 'The practice of postcoloniality: a pedagogy of hope', *Pedagogy, Culture & Society*, 14(3): 279–293.

Lewin, K.M. (2007) 'Diversity in convergence: access to education for all', *Compare*, 37(5): 577–599.

Lopes Cardozo, M.T.A. (2012) 'Decolonising Bolivian education: ideology versus reality', in T.G. Griffiths and Z. Millei (eds) *Logics of Socialist Education: Engaging with Crisis, Insecurity and Uncertainty*, Zurich: Springer, pp 21–35.

Maldonado-Torres, N. (2007) 'On coloniality of being: contributions to the development of a concept', *Cultural Studies*, 21(2–2): 240–270.

Mamdani, M. (1996) *Citizen and Subject: Contemporary Africa and the Legacy of Late Colonialism*, Princeton, NJ: Princeton University Press.

Mbembe, A. (2016) 'Decolonizing the university: new directions', *Arts and Humanities in Higher Education*, 15(1): 29–45.

Mbembe, A. and Posel, D. (2005) 'A critical humanism', *Interventions: International Journal of Postcolonial Studies*, 7(3): 283–286.

Mignolo, W.D. (2011) 'Geopolitics of sensing and knowing: on (de)coloniality, border thinking and epistemic disobedience', *Postcolonial Studies*, 14(3): 273–283.

Mignolo, W.D. and Walsh, C. (2018) *On Decoloniality: Concepts, Analytics, Praxis*, New York: Duke University Press.

Ministry of Education and Vocational Training (2018) 'Education Sector Development Plan (ESDP) 2016/17–2020/21', Dar es Salaam: MoEVT.

REFERENCES

Mitchell, R. (2017) 'An ethnographic case study of the agendas, participation and influence of stakeholders at an urban government primary school in Tigray, Ethiopia', Unpublished doctoral dissertation, University of Leicester.

Mohan, G. (2013) 'Beyond the enclave: towards a critical political economy of China in Africa', *Development and Change*, 44(6): 1255–1272.

Moon, B. (2012) *Teacher Education and the Challenge of Development*, London: Routledge.

Morrell, E. and Rowsell, J. (2019) *Stories from Inequity to Justice in Literacy Education*, Abingdon: Routledge.

Mulkeen, A. (2005) 'Teachers for rural schools: a challenge for Africa', in *Ministerial Seminar on Education for Rural People in Africa: Policy Lessons, Options and Priorities*, 21 July 2005, Addis Ababa: FAO, UNESCO IIEP, ADEA.

Mulkeen, A. (2010) *Teachers in Anglophone Africa: Issues in Teacher Supply, Training, and Management*, Washington, DC: World Bank.

Mulkeen, A., Chapman, D., DeJaeghere, J. and Leu, E. (2007) *Recruiting, Retaining, and Retraining Secondary School Teachers and Principals in Sub-Saharan Africa*, World Bank Working Papers, pp 1–96.

Mulugeta, A. and Gebregziabher, M. (2022) 'Saving children from man-made acute malnutrition in Tigray, Ethiopia: a call to action', *The Lancet Global Health*, 10(4): e469–e470.

Musisi, S. and Kinyanda, E. (2020) 'Long-term impact of war, civil war, and persecution in civilian populations – conflict and post-traumatic stress in African communities', *Frontiers in Psychiatry*, 11: 20.

Mwoma, T. and Pillay, J. (2015) 'Psychosocial support for orphans and vulnerable children in public primary schools: challenges and intervention strategies', *South African Journal of Education*, 35(3), https://doi.org/10.15700/saje.v35n3a1092.

Nchimbi, A. (2018) 'The trade unions performance in Tanzania: the perceptions of school teachers union in Singida Municipality', *Open Journal of Social Sciences*, 6(4): 242–254.

Ndlovu-Gatsheni, S. (2013) *Coloniality of Power in Postcolonial Africa: Myths of Decolonization*, Senegal: CODESRIA.

Ndlovu-Gatsheni, S.J. (2015) 'Decoloniality as the future of Africa', *History Compass*, 13(10): 485–496.

Nias, J. (1989) 'Subjectively speaking: English primary teachers' careers', *International Journal of Educational Research*, 13(4): 391–402.

Nkrumah, K. (1966) *Neo-colonialism: The Last Stage of Imperialism*, London: Thomas Nelson and Sons.

Novelli, M. (2010) 'Education, conflict and social (in)justice: insights from Colombia', *Educational Review*, 62(3): 271–285.

Novelli, M. and Sayed, Y. (2016) 'Teachers as agents of sustainable peace, social cohesion and development: theory, practice and evidence', *Education as Change*, 20: 15–37.

Novelli, M. and Higgins, S. (2017) 'The violence of peace and the role of education: insights from Sierra Leone', *Compare: A Journal of Comparative and International Education*, 47(1): 32–45.

Novelli, M., Lopes Cardozo, M. and Smith, A. (2019) 'The "4 Rs" as a tool for critical policy analysis of the education sector in conflict affected states', *Education and Conflict Review*, 2: 70–75.

Nussbaum, M. (2000) *Women and Development: The Capabilities Approach*, Cambridge: Cambridge University Press.

Nussbaum, M.C. (2011) *Creating Capabilities*, Cambridge, MA: Harvard University Press.

Nyerere, J. (1967) *Education for Self-Reliance*, [online]. Available from: www.jstor.org/stable/24457417 [Accessed 20 December 2023].

Oumer, J. (2009) *The Challenges of Free Primary Education in Ethiopia*, Paris: UNESCO, IIEP (International Institute for Educational Planning).

Parkes, J. (2015) 'Gender Based Violence in Education', Brighton: University of Sussex.

Paulson, J., Abiti, N., Osorio, J., Hernández, C., Keo, D., Manning, P. et al (2020) 'Education as site of memory: developing a research agenda', *International Studies in Sociology of Education*, 29(4): 429–451.

Pearson, P. (2013) 'Policy without a plan: English as a medium of instruction in Rwanda', *Current Issues in Language Planning*, 15: 39–56.

REFERENCES

Peñuela Contreras, D.M. and Rodríguez Murcia, V.M. (2006) 'Pedagogical movement: other forms of educational resistance', *Folios*, (23): 3–14. Available at: https://revistas.pedagogica.edu.co/index.php/RF/article/view/10185 [Accessed 19 January 2024].

Perry, K. (2020a) 'The new "Bond-Age", climate crisis and the case for climate reparations: unpicking old/new colonialities of finance for development within the SDGs', *SSRN Electronic Journal*, 10.2139/ssrn.3739103.

Perry, K. (2020b) 'Structuralism and human development: a seamless marriage? An assessment of poverty, production and environmental challenges in CARICOM countries', *International Journal of Political Economy*, 49(3): 222–242.

Pesambili, J.C., Sayed, Y. and Stambach, A. (2022) 'The World Bank's construction of teachers and their work: a critical analysis', *International Journal of Educational Development*, 92: 102609.

Pritchett, L. (2013) *The Rebirth of Education: Schooling Ain't Learning*, Washington, DC: Centre for Global Development.

Probyn, M. (2015) 'Pedagogical translanguaging: bridging discourses in South African science classrooms', *Language and Education*, 29(3): 218–234.

Pryor, J., Akyeampong, K., Westbrook, J. and Lussier, K. (2012) 'Rethinking teacher preparation and professional development in Africa: an analysis of the curriculum of teacher education in the teaching of early reading and mathematics', *The Curriculum Journal*, 23(4): 409–502.

Quijano, A. (2000) 'Coloniality of power and Eurocentrism in Latin America', *International Sociology*, 15(2): 215–232.

Quijano, A. (2007) 'Coloniality and modernity/rationality', *Cultural Studies*, 21(2–3): 168–178.

Robertson, S.L. (2012) 'Placing teachers in global governance agendas', *Comparative Education Review*, 56(4): 584–607.

Robertson, S.L., Novelli, M., Dale, R., Tikly, L., Dachi, H. and Ndibalema, A. (2007) *Globalisation, Education and Development: Ideas, Actors and Dynamics*, London: Department for International Development.

Robeyns, I. (2017) *Wellbeing, Freedom and Social Justice: The Capability Approach Re-Examined*, Cambridge: Open Book Publishers.

Rodney, W. (1973) *How Europe Underdeveloped Africa*, London: Bogle-L'Ouverture Publications.

Rwanda (Institute of Policy Analysis and Research) (2014) 'Evaluation of Results Based Aid in Rwandan Education: 2013 Evaluation Report', London: DfID.

Sachs, J. (2001) 'Teacher professional identity: competing discourses, competing outcomes', *Journal of Education Policy*, 16(2): 149–161.

Santos, De Sousa (2012) 'The Public Sphere and Epistemologies of the South', *African Development*, XXXVI(1): 43–68.

Sayed, Y. et al (2018) 'The Role of Teachers in Peacebuilding and Social Cohesion in Rwanda and South Africa', ESRC/DFID Research Report, University of Sussex, UK.

Schon, D.A. (1991) *The Reflective Practitioner: How Professionals Think in Action*, Abingdon: Routledge.

Sen, A. (1999) *Development as Freedom*, Oxford: Oxford University Press.

Sen, A. (2011) *The Idea of Justice*, Cambridge, MA: Harvard University Press.

Shahjahan, R.A., Estera, A.L., Surla, K.L. and Edwards, K.T. (2021) ' "Decolonizing" curriculum and pedagogy: a comparative review across disciplines and global higher education contexts', *Review of Educational Research*, https://doi.org/10.3102/0034654321 1042423.

Shulman, L. (2011) 'Knowledge and teaching: foundations of the new reform', *Harvard Educational Review*, 57(1): 1–23.

Speed, S. (2017) 'Structures of settler capitalism in Abya Yala', *American Quarterly*, 69(4): 783–790.

Stephen, M.D. (2014) 'Rising powers, global capitalism and liberal global governance: a historical materialist account of the BRICs challenge', *European Journal of International Relations*, 20(4): 912–938.

Taddese, E.T. and Rao, C. (2021) 'Teachers' professional learning practices in the workplace: experiences of primary school teachers in Ethiopia', *Education*, 3–13, https://doi.org/10.1080/03004 279.2021.1973531.

REFERENCES

Takayama, K., Sriprakash, A. and Connell, R. (2015) 'Rethinking knowledge production and circulation in comparative and international education: southern theory, postcolonial perspectives, and alternative epistemologies', *Comparative Education Review*, 59(1), https://doi.org/10.1086/679660.

Tao, S. (2014) 'Using the capability approach to improve female teacher deployment to rural schools in Nigeria', *International Journal of Educational Development*, 39: 92–99.

Teka, E. (2021) 'Progress of the war', in H. Hagos and K. Tronvoll (eds) *The Tigray War and Regional Implications*, Eritrea Focus: Oslo Analytica.

Thiong'o, N. (1986) *Decolonising the Mind: The Politics of Language in African Literature*, London: James Currey.

Tigray Education Bureau (2021) Summary Report of Human and Material Damage on Tigray's Education, Mekelle-Ethiopia.

Tikly, L. (2004) 'Education and the new imperialism', *Comparative Education*, 40(2): 173–198.

Tikly, L. (2013) 'Reconceptualizing TVET and development: a human capability and social justice approach', *Revisiting Global Trends in TVET: Reflections on Theory*, Paris: UNESCO.

Tikly, L. (2017) 'The future of Education for All as a global regime of educational governance', *Comparative Education Review*, 61(1): 22–57.

Tikly, L. (2020) *Education for Sustainable Development in the Postcolonial World: Towards a Transformative Agenda for Africa*, Abingdon: Routledge.

Tikly, L. and Barrett, A. (2011) 'Social justice, capabilities and the quality of education in low income countries', *International Journal of Educational Development*, 31(1): 3–14.

Tikly, L. and Barrett, A. (2013) *Education Quality and Social Justice in the Global South: Challenges for Policy, Practice and Research*, Abingdon: Routledge.

Tikly, L., Barrett, A., Batra, P., Bernal, A., Cameron, L., Coles, A. et al (2023) *Decolonising Teacher Professionalism: Foregrounding the Perspectives of Teachers in the Global South*. Background paper prepared for the *UNESCO Futures of Teaching Initiative*. Paris: UNESCO, https://doi.org/10.5281/zenodo.7097105.

Tiruneh, D., Sabates, R. and Woldehanna, T. (2021) 'Disadvantaged schools and students in Ethiopia: why is the GEQIP-E reform necessary?', 2021/026, https://doi.org/10.35489/BSG-RISE-RI_2021/026.

Tolon, C. (2014) *Teacher Experiences during the Shift in Medium of Instruction in Rwanda: Voices from Kigali Public Schools*, Brighton: University of Sussex.

Triulzi, A. (1982) 'Italian colonialism and Ethiopia', *Journal of African History*, 23(2): 237–243.

UIS (2006) *Teachers and Educational Quality: Monitoring Global Needs for 2015*, Montreal: UNESCO Institute for Statistics.

UIS (2012) 'UIS Information Bulletin No.9: School and Teaching Resources in Sub-Saharan Africa, Analysis of the 2011 UIS Regional Data Collection on Education', Toronto: UNESCO Institute for Statistics (UIS).

UN (2022) 'Ethiopia: civilians again mired in intractable and deadly war, Human Rights Council hears', UN News, [online] September. Available from: https://news.un.org/en/story/2022/09/1127481 [Accessed 17 January 2023].

UNESCO (2004) 'Education for All – The Quality Imperative', Paris: UNESCO.

UNESCO (2014) 'EFA Global Monitoring Report – 2013–2014 – Teaching and Learning Achieving Quality for All', Paris: UNESCO.

UNESCO (2015) 'Education for All 2000–2015: Achievements and Challenges', Paris: UNESCO.

UNESCO (2017) 'Global Education Monitoring Report: Accountability in Education: Meeting Our Commitments', Paris: UNESCO.

UNESCO (2019) 'Behind the Numbers: Ending School Violence and Bullying', Paris: UNESCO.

UNESCO (2020) 'Significant Efforts by Colombia Ensure That Nearly 200,000 Venezuelan Children and Youth Have Access to the Educational System', Paris: UNESCO.

UNESCO/EI (2019) 'Global Framework of Professional Teaching Standards', Paris: UNESCO.

REFERENCES

UNESCO/UIS (2019) 'New Methodology Shows That 258 Million Children, Adolescents and Youth Are Out of School', Paris: UNESCO.

UNESCO/UIS (2021) 'Pandemic-Related Disruptions to Schooling and Impacts on Learning Proficiency Indicators: A Focus on the Early Grades', New York: UNICEF.

UNICEF (2015) 'Corporal Punishment in Schools', New York: UNICEF.

UNICEF (2020) 'COVID-19 and Child Labour: A Time of Crisis, a Time to Act', New York: UNICEF.

UNOCHA (United Nations Office for the Coordination of African Affairs) (2021) *Ethiopia – Tigray Region Update*, [online]. Available from https://reports.unocha.org/en/country/ethiopia/ [Accessed 26 August 2023].

Verger, A., Fontdevila, C. and Zancajo, A. (2016) *The Privatization of Education: A Political Economy of Global Education Reform*, New York: Teachers College Press.

Voce, A., Leylan, C. and Michael, C. (2021) ' "Cultural genocide": the shameful history of Canada's residential schools – mapped', *The Guardian*, 6 September.

Walker, M. and Unterhalter, E. (2007) *Amartya Sen's Capability Approach and Social Justice in Education*, New York: Palgrave Macmillan.

Walsh, C. (2007) 'Shifting the geopolitics of critical knowledge', *Cultural Studies*, 21(2–3): 224–239.

Walsh, C.E. (2015) 'Decolonial pedagogies walking and asking. Notes to Paulo Freire from AbyaYala', *International Journal of Lifelong Education*, 34(1): 9–21.

Weigele, A. and Brandt, C.O. (2022) ' "Just keep silent". Teaching under the control of authoritarian governments: a qualitative study of government schools in Addis Ababa, Ethiopia', *International Journal of Educational Development*, 88: 102497.

Welmond, M. (2002) 'Globalization viewed from the periphery: the dynamics of teacher identity in the Republic of Benin', *Comparative Education Review*, 46(1): 37–65.

Westbrook, J., Brown, N., Orr, D., Pryor, J. and Salvi, J. (2013) 'Pedagogy, Curriculum, Teaching Practices and Teacher Education in Developing Countries', London: DfID.

Whitty, G. (2008) 'Changing modes of teacher professionalism: traditional, managerial, collaborative and democratic', in B. Cunningham (ed) *Exploring Professionalism*, London: Institute of Education, University of London, pp 28–49.

Woods, P. and Jeffrey, B. (2002) 'The reconstruction of primary teachers' identities', *British Journal of Sociology of Education*, 23(1): 89–106.

World Bank (2022) 'World Bank supports Ethiopia's conflict-affected communities, targets over five million people', Press Release, [online] 12 April. Available from: www.worldbank.org/en/news/press-release/2022/04/12/world-bank-supports-ethiopia-s-conflict-affected-communities-targets-over-five-million-people [Accessed 6 January 2024].

World Vision (2020) 'COVID-19 Aftershocks: A Perfect Storm: Millions More Children at Risk of Violence under Lockdown and into the "New Normal"', London: World Vision.

Zanotti, L. (2021) *Exploring Agency and Resistance in the Context of Global Entanglements*, Abingdon: Routledge.

Index

References to endnotes show both the
page number and the note number (91n2)

A

accountability 15, 22
administrative work, teachers'
    36–37
Africa 29, 31, 35, 53–54, 62, 63,
    72, 88
armed conflicts 4, 12, 29, 33, 65
    see also Tigray, impact of civil
    war in
assessments
    under colonialism 36
    evaluation of teachers by their
        students 44
    high-stakes, performance of
        learners in 24
autonomy 16, 18, 22, 25, 36,
    37–38, 44, 50–51, 68, 69, 74

B

boarding schools 27
Bolivia 6
BRICS 29

C

Canada 31
capability approach 25, 70
capitalism 31, 46
Central Institute of Education
    Literacy Group (Delhi
    University) 58
China 24, 34
civil servants 19, 37, 42
class sizes 39, 40–42, 41
collective professionalism 17
collegiality 18, 52, 73

Colombia 6, 9, 12, 89
    and coloniality of being 63–65
    and coloniality of knowledge
        49–50, 54–55, 57–58
    and coloniality of power 29–30,
        33, 35–36, 38–39, 41–42
    European colonization of 29
    Movimiento Pedagógico 26,
        38–39, 42
    pedagogical movement, teachers'
        role in 26
    Todos a aprender (Let's All
        Learn) 58–59
coloniality of being 5, 28, 61, 74
    emotional rewards 65–66
    and salaries 61–63
    societal and systemic
        problems 63–65
coloniality of knowledge 4–5, 28,
    46–47, 68, 69, 74
    and curricula 47–51
    and digitization 53–57
    and languages 51–53
    and teacher education 57–60
    teachers as innovators 60
coloniality of power 4, 28–30
    and class 40–42
    global agendas and national
        education policy 39–40
    and modern education
        systems 31–39
    and privatization of
        education 42–45
community leaders, teachers as 72
comparative education 3
conflicts
    armed 4, 12, 29, 33, 65

effects on young people 83–84
impact of 33, 69
see also Tigray, impact of civil war in
continuing professional
development (CPD) 58–59
corporal punishment 26
corporate employees, teachers as 22
CoSCAR approach 9–10
COVID-19 pandemic, impact
of 1, 4, 12, 13–14, 37, 40,
44–45, 53, 68, 71
creolization 29
cultural mediators, teachers as
69–70, 72
curricula 5, 7, 26, 28, 46–47, 57,
59, 60, 72
arts and culture in 49
centralized 72
colonial 47
competency-based 40, 48
decontextualized and
irrelevant 47–51, 63
'Happiness Curriculum' 50
and liberalism 43
outcomes-based 48
pandemic's impact on 50
perceived lack of relevance
of 49, 57–58
standardization of 49–50
subject-based 48
and teachers' autonomy 18, 22,
36, 38
vocationalization of 48

D

digital inequalities 56–57
digitization of teaching and
learning 53–57

E

EdTech 54, 56
Education for All (EFA) 1, 15, 19,
35, 63
Education International 15, 20, 71
education quality 1, 15, 20, 24,
38–38, 39, 42, 54, 70, 72, 73, 86

education systems
bureaucracy, and teachers' pay 37
colonial 35, 37
mass 7, 28, 66
of state, under-resourced 35–36
education workforce, mobilization
of 85–86
emotional rewards of teaching 65–66
endogenous privatization of
education 43
Ethiopia 2, 12, 29
automatic promotion policy 41
and coloniality of being 62, 64
and coloniality of knowledge 52,
54, 58–59
and coloniality of power 29–30,
36–37, 43–44
Tigray *see* Tigray, impact of civil
war in
Eurocentric models 1, 2, 5, 7, 10,
28, 46
everyday realities 28, 61
see also coloniality of being
expertise of teachers 18, 20, 70, 71
exploitation 13, 25, 26, 31, 57

F

FECODE (teachers' union) 38–39
financial crisis 2008, impact of 42

G

Global Framework of Professional
Teaching Standards 20
global teachers' organizations 15
government policy 17, 23
and global agendas 39–40
and teachers' autonomy 37–38,
39, 68, 73

H

higher education 7, 17–18, 50

I

India 2, 6, 9, 11, 23, 89, 91
and coloniality of being 62, 64

INDEX

and coloniality of knowledge 50, 54–56, 58, 60
and coloniality of power 29–30, 35–38, 41–42
DIKSHA (Government of India portal) 60
European colonization of 29
modern education system 47–48
monitoring of teachers by school inspectors 44–45
National Council for Educational Research and Training (NCERT) 60
National Curriculum Framework 2005 60
New Education Policy 42–43
school inspectors, monitoring of teachers by 44–45, 50
indigenous and local knowledge 2, 7, 31, 47, 48
indigenous elites 30, 31, 32
infrastructure, educational 40, 77, 79–83, 86–87
innovators, teachers as 60
International Labour Organization (ILO) 15, 17
International Monetary Fund (IMF) 23
international non-governmental organizations (INGOs) 15
international organizations (IOs) 13, 23, 34

J

Jomtien conference (1990) 40

K

knowledge 1, 16, 18, 20, 22, 61, 63, 66, 71, 72
co-creation 8, 11
indigenous and local 7, 26, 48
of teaching 21
Western 2, 7, 47
see also coloniality of knowledge

L

languages 51–53, 72
Latin America 6, 29, 35
Liberia 87
low fee private schools (LFPS) 42

M

management-driven professionalism 22–25
migrations 33, 41
Millennium Development Goals (MDGs) 39, 40
modern education systems 30, 47
and coloniality of power 31–34
emergence of 34–39
multi-grade classrooms 41

N

native populations, exploitation and enslavement of 31
Ndlovu-Gatsheni, S.J. 3–4, 6, 28, 31–32, 46, 61
neocolonialism 31–32, 39
neoliberalism 22, 34, 42, 43, 73
neo-patrimonial state 32
Nkrumah, K. 31
Nyerere, J. 47

O

oppression 25, 26, 27
Organisation for Co-operation and Economic Development Programme for International Student Assessment (OECD's PISA) 23, 50
out-of-school learning 64

P

para-teachers 15, 43
parents–communities relationships 73
pedagogy 20, 22, 28, 38, 53, 60, 68, 72
performance management techniques 43, 44

Plasma TV, as teaching aid 53–54
power 17
  colonial matrix of 3, 7
  geopolitical 3
  see also coloniality of power
primary schooling, access to 40
principles for improving teacher
  professionalism (World
  Bank) 24
privatization of education 23, 32,
  42–45, 68
Programme for International
  Student Assessment (OECD's
  PISA) 23, 50
public training programmes 58

R

*Recommendation Concerning
  the Status of Teachers* (ILO/
  UNESCO, 1966) 17–18, 19, 22
redistribution 32, 88
refugee children 12, 33, 41
relationships 21, 55–56, 73
responsibility 16, 18, 22, 65–66
#RhodesMustFall 6
rights-based approach, to teacher
  professionalism 4, 15, 17–21,
  25, 68
Rwanda 2, 9, 11, 29
  and coloniality of being 62, 64
  and coloniality of knowledge 52,
  54, 58–59
  and coloniality of power 29–30,
  36, 38

S

salaries of teachers 23, 26, 37,
  42–44, 61–63, 68, 73, 79,
  85–86
semi-professions 16
Sen, A. 25, 70
sexual harassment 27
situating teacher professionalism
  17, 27, 67–70
social justice approach, to teacher
  professionalism 16, 25–27

social media 53, 60
social recognition 18
societal and systemic
  problems 63–65
state expenditure on education 42
structural adjustment 19, 23,
  39, 42
student movements 6
sub-Saharan Africa 54
*Successful Teachers, Successful
  Students: Recruiting and
  Supporting Society's Most Crucial
  Profession* 23–24
surveillance of teachers 22, 44–45,
  55, 73
Sustainable Development Goals
  (SDGs) 1, 2, 19–20, 39

T

Tanzania 2, 9, 12, 26, 29
  and coloniality of being 62
  and coloniality of knowledge
  47–49, 52–54, 57, 60
  and coloniality of power 29–30,
  35, 37–38, 40–42, 44
  Education for Self-Reliance 47
  Ujamaa 26
teacher education 3, 5, 9, 27, 43,
  57–60
teacher governance 68
teacher training 39, 47, 57,
  60, 86
teacher–learner relationships 55
teachers' unions and professional
  associations 33, 37, 38
teaching, comparisons with other
  professions 16
teaching knowledge and
  understanding *see* knowledge
teaching practices 21, 50, 58, 60,
  71–73
teaching relations *see* relationships
technologies, new 59–60
  see also digitization of teaching
  and learning
textbooks, colonial 47

INDEX

Tigray, impact of civil war in 4–6, 12, 33, 64–65, 76–77
  experiences of trauma 79–83
  post-conflict reconstruction 85
  reimagining schooling 87–88
  school buildings as IDP shelters 81
  school infrastructure devastation of 79–83
  reconstruction of 86–87
  teachers as civilians 77–79
Trends In International Mathematics and Science Study (TIMMS) 50

U

UNESCO 15, 20
  Futures of the Teaching Profession Initiative 1, 91n1
  UNESCO/IE model 71

V

Venezuela 12, 33, 41
violence 26
  in education 27
  sexualized and gender-based 26
  see also conflicts; Tigray, impact of civil war in
voices of teachers
  and feedback system 38
  in policy-making processes 37–38, 39, 68, 73

W

Westphalian model 32, 91n2
#WhyIsMyCurriculumWhite 6
World Bank 15, 22–25, 34, 42, 67–68, 70, 87